CHELTENHAM IN ANTARCTICA

THE LIFE OF EDWARD WILSON

D.M. WILSON
&
D.B. ELDER

*****

Three mottoes have helped me and are good to live with:

Wilson motto - Res Non Verba (Do, and don't talk);
Cheltenham College motto - Labor Omnia Vincit (Work overcomes everything);
Caius College motto - Labor Ipse Voluptas (Work is its own joy).

EAW
*****

All of the royalties from this book will benefit the Wilson Collection Fund at the Cheltenham Art Gallery and Museums, which helps to preserve the Wilson Family Archive.

Published
by
REARDON PUBLISHING
56, Upper Norwood Street
Cheltenham, GL53 0DU
England
www.reardon.co.uk

Written and Researched
by
D.M. Wilson & D.B. Elder

Copyright © 2000

ISBN 1 873877 45 5

Design and Layout
by
D.M. Wilson & N. Reardon

Walks Recreated
by
D.B. Elder

Printed
by
Stoate and Bishop Ltd
Cheltenham

Introduction

Edward Adrian Wilson is perhaps the most famous native son of Cheltenham. In the early years of the 20th Century, he was one of the major influences and personalities of the heroic age of Antarctic exploration and has also been recognised as one of the top ranking ornithologists and naturalists in the United Kingdom during this period. He was also one of the last great scientific expedition artists.

Despite this, remarkably little has been published about him. His father wrote an unpublished biography of him shortly after his death. This was an important source for George Seaver, who published three volumes of biography on Edward Wilson in the 1930s and 40s, fortunately quoting extensively from his letters and diaries. After the appearance of the first two volumes much of the source material that Seaver had used was destroyed, most of it on the instructions of Oriana, Edward Wilson's widow. There was nothing malicious in this: she simply thought that she had done her public duty in allowing a biography to be published and did not want strangers digging around in her private correspondence after her death. In the 1960s and 70s, through the Scott Polar Research Institute, the Antarctic expedition diaries of Edward Wilson and a volume of his Antarctic bird pictures were published. Several people tried to write new biographies in the 1970s and 80s but all failed for the lack of new material: due to the subsequent events, George Seaver's books and the published diaries already contained much of the source material about the life of Edward Wilson.

As such this volume draws heavily on the work of Edward Wilson's father, on the published diaries, and on George Seaver. With Seaver in particular, however, his use of the historical sources available to him requires a word of caution: he frequently used the narrative technique of rolling quotations from several letters or diary entries into one quotation, passing them off as a single quotation from a single document. Since he published no footnotes it is almost impossible to establish where he has or has not done this, although his longer quotations, or quotations from complete letters, tend to be accurate. Unlike some commentators in subsequent generations, who often use quotation techniques to alter historical facts and to mis-represent what was said, with Seaver it is generally benign - he has not, as far as we have discovered, changed the sense of meaning, or mis-represented facts external to the actual form of the quotation. It is, however, something of a disaster from the point of view of accurate scholarship given that the original manuscripts are often no longer available. We have done our best, where possible, to find the original sources but these are very scattered, where they still exist, and it is painstaking work. Occasionally, they can be recreated through bringing together copied extracts - fortunately a habit in which many of the Wilson family indulged - such as in Edward Wilson's last letter to Oriana, reproduced towards the end of this book.

In many ways, therefore, the following text should not be seen as a major new biography of Edward Wilson but rather as a complement to the volumes of George Seaver. This is not to say that there is no new material in the book, there should be enough to interest polar scholars, though there may not be as much as they had hoped. Where possible, we have also chosen to use previously unpublished illustrations from the vast collections of Edward Wilson's pictures. These, alone, should be enough to interest those in search of new material. Our aim, however, is to meet the many hundreds of enquiries received about this famous son of Cheltenham and his life. Edward Wilson is one of the most asked after aspects of the collections at the Cheltenham Art Gallery and Museums. This work is intended to answer this demand from the public for something about Edward Wilson to be available to them in print, and to identify the 'Wilson sites' in and around Cheltenham, rather than to write an academic book. As such there are no footnotes but an annotated copy of the text will be placed in the collections of the Scott Polar Research Institute, the Cheltenham Public Library and the Cheltenham Museum, so that those who may be interested in the historical sources for this work will be able to find them.

Finally, it seems impossible not to say a few words about the contemporary situation as regards polar historical scholarship and biography, against which this book will inevitably be judged by some. We hope that this work is an exception to the current fashion for cynicism. Some will doubtless find it an "old fashioned" or "non-critical" work as a result. For this we make no apology. Our aim isn't to pick for faults like vultures at a carcass, nor to sit in judgement, but to help you to get to know a remarkably complex man a little better - and maybe - just maybe - you will find a little inspiration for your own life and times through the life and times of Edward Adrian Wilson.

D. M. Wilson and D. B. Elder
October 2000.

Authors' Notes:

In keeping with the historical period, all units of measurement are given in imperial values with the metric conversion following in brackets. Unless otherwise stated, distances within the biographical text are given in geographical (or nautical) miles. One geographical mile is equivalent to 1.15 statute miles or 1.85 kilometres. In the Wilson Walk maps at the end, regular statute miles are used.

In keeping with Edward Wilson's lifetime habit of annotating books, letters and his diaries with sketches and with private thoughts summarising meaning, we have chosen to insert some of his sketches - or occasionally details of larger pictures - into the text and to start each chapter with an extract from his writings, which we hope will give some appropriate reflection of his thinking.

Acknowledgements

We would like to acknowledge the considerable kindness of the numerous individuals and institutions that have assisted in the production of this book in many different ways. If we were to acknowledge everybody who has helped us it would fill a small book in itself - but we are genuinely very grateful to you all, particularly those hard pressed individuals in under-funded public institutions whose time is always over-stretched. We would also like to thank the numerous individuals and private collectors who have permitted us to reproduce material from their collections, whether through the use of quotations or the reproduction of pictures. In a similar vein, we also wish to thank all of the following institutions for their permission to reproduce material from their collections: The Scott Polar Research Institute, Cambridge (SPRI); Cheltenham Art Gallery and Museums (CAGM); Cheltenham Public Library (CL); The Headmaster, and the Cheltonian Society, of Cheltenham College (CC); The Master and Fellows of Gonville and Caius College, Cambridge; The Natural History Museum, London (NHM); and the publishers, John Murray, for permission to use material from the biographies of Edward Wilson by George Seaver.

In addition the following individuals have helped us enormously by reading parts of the text and giving their advice: R. K. Headland F.R.G.S. the Archivist and Curator at the Scott Polar Research Institute; Dr S. Blake, Keeper of Collections at the Cheltenham Museum; the polar historian, D. E. Yelverton F.R.G.S.; D. C. Lawie F.R.S.A.; and Mrs A. Elder (née Gauld). We would also like to thank Mrs S. Pierce and Mrs E. Gemmill for their hard work, particularly as regards reading the proofs. Needless to say, none of the above are responsible for the contents of the book in any way.

Finally, we would like to acknowledge the long sufferance of our immediate families, Meg, Rachel, Catrin and Duncan - who supported us all the way.

1. "A Queer Little Character"

Tuesday 23 July 1872 dawned warm and cloudy in Cheltenham. At number six Montpellier Terrace, the serenity of the day was punctuated by the fuss of the midwife and house servants. Here, in the large front bedroom on the first landing, was born the second son and fifth child of Edward Thomas Wilson and Mary Agnes (née Whishaw). The expanding family of a local physician, if an influential one in local civic life, drew little comment in the press. They were more concerned with the thunderstorms and floods which were to deluge Cheltenham in the ensuing days. Yet nearly 41 years later, at the news of his death, the name of this child, Edward Adrian Wilson, would be known across the length and breadth of the British Empire and beyond.

He was born into a flourishing family, full of strong, colourful characters, with a typically Victorian sense of the family and its lineage. On his father's side the Wilson family stretched back into 17th century Westmoreland and descended from a long line of Quakers, although there hadn't been a Quaker in direct descent for three generations by the time Edward Adrian was born. The last had been his great grandfather, Edward Wilson of Liverpool and Philadelphia (1772-1843), who had made a fortune through land in America and the birth of the railways. He was a friend of George Stevenson's, a director of the Liverpool and Manchester Railway and one of the few people to successfully reclaim lands in the United States after the War of Independence. The children inherited fortunes and wrote 'Gentleman' as their occupation; they were inveterate collectors and were major benefactors of public institutions on more than one continent. They were fascinated by the world around them. Edward Wilson of Hean Castle (1808-1888) ('Grandfather') was one of these. He brought together what was reputed to be one of the finest collections of hummingbirds in existence. He became High Sheriff of Pembrokeshire in 1861 and was a widely respected landowner. A series of poor investments meant that the next generation did not inherit fortunes but were merely wealthy, becoming adventurers and pioneers. Two of his sons ('Uncle Henry' and 'Uncle Rathmel') spent time in the Argentine where one lost an eye to a lasso. Another son, Major General Sir Charles Wilson ('Uncle Charlie'), rose to become a famous explorer of the Middle East and was a key figure in the attempted rescue of Gordon from Khartoum. His books are in print to this day. The eldest son, however, who was to become known to subsequent generations as ETW, was known to Edward Adrian simply as 'Dad'. Edward Thomas Wilson of

Cheltenham (1832-1918), was a Fellow of the Royal College of Physicians. He had declined fame and fortune in the London hospitals, choosing instead to become a general practitioner and consultant in Cheltenham from 1859. Here he pioneered modern medical practices, such as clean drinking water, isolation fever hospitals and district nurses. He was President of the local Natural Science Society and helped to found the Delancey Hospital and the local Municipal Museum.

On his mother's side, the Whishaw family stretched back into 16th century Cheshire and descended from a long line of successful lawyers and businessmen. This branch of the Whishaw family had made its home amongst the expatriate English community in St. Petersburg with many connections, and rumours of blood ties, into the Russian Imperial House. His grandfather Bernhard Whishaw (1779-1868) married Elizabeth Yeames (1796-1879), also from a powerful expatriate English family in St. Petersburg. Having founded one of the most successful Anglo-Russian trading companies, they moved to Cheltenham around 1850. Elizabeth went to great lengths to dominate Cheltenham Society. Many of the family (uncles and aunts) stayed behind or returned to reside in Russia. Here, amongst the English expatriate trading community, they enjoyed the personal protection of Tsar Nicholas I during the Crimean War and would take evening strolls with him along the quays of St. Petersburg. They spent the summers in their country Dachas hunting and fishing; an association and way of life that was brought to a close in 1917 when some of them would flee from the Russian Revolution through Norway and travel past a monument to the memory of Edward Adrian. The youngest child of Bernhard and Elizabeth, however, came with them to Cheltenham at the age of seven and lived there for the rest of her life. Mary Agnes Wilson, née Whishaw, (1841-1930) was energetic and forthright. A good horse rider and a keen gardener, she also enjoyed painting and reading theological books. More importantly, perhaps, she was a respected authority on the breeding of poultry, the first to import and breed Plymouth Rocks from America and the author of the *ABC of Poultry* (1880), which was considered a definitive work for many years. She was known to Edward Adrian simply as 'Mother'.

This was the sort of family that hired a shop window to watch the first motor cars race through Cheltenham at eight miles an hour. Moreover, it was figures such as these who filled the family stories of Edward Adrian's childhood. Tales of Empire, exploration and wild adventures in the far flung corners of the globe widened his eyes with impish delight. It gave him the inheritance of an enquiring mind, the inspiration for living life to the full and the privilege of a strong sense of belonging. It was also figures such as these who gathered at the home of his paternal grandparents on 16 September 1872 for his baptism. He was baptised by Canon Stephenson in St. John's Church, Weymouth: Edward, after the line of his paternal forebears and Adrian after a relative on his paternal grandmother's side. In the family, however, he became universally known as Ted.

With deep red hair and a ready smile, Ted was regarded by his mother as "the prettiest of all my babies". At eleven months he could take steps alone and was soon running and climbing over everything, speaking his first words ("papa" and "mama") and spreading mayhem in the wake of his violent outbursts of temper. His parents nevertheless took their traditional one month holiday away from the family during the summer of 1873, leaving the children in charge of the nurse, and on this occasion visiting family members in Russia. At Christmas, Ted joined his older siblings in the family tradition of the singing of carols for their parents whilst they prepared for Church. Later, Father Christmas appeared, as he did every year, following the unfortunate calling away of ETW on 'an urgent medical emergency'. Ted received the gift of a model farmyard and a trumpet, with which he doubtless continued his terrorisation of the nursery.

During this period the Wilson family was still growing, both in physical numbers and in stature, with ETW'S growing reputation as a physician. Both led to the requirement for a larger house. In September 1874 they moved around the corner to *Westal* on Montpellier Parade. *Westal* was a large, detached 'Regency' house, with a private carriage sweep, large gardens and stabling, greenhouses and ferneries, marble fire places, four reception rooms, ten bedrooms, a nursery and servants' quarters. The requirements of the household meant that five servants were employed in the house alone - not untypical of the period. With *Westal* they inherited 'Tom', a large grey cat with a severed tail, "a redoubtable mouser and general family pet". The story was that he had been a favourite cat at Dowdeswell Court, so his tail was cut off in order that the gamekeeper might recognise him and spare his life.

For many years, and for all Ted's life, *Westal* was the Wilson family home. It was here at the age of three that he gave performances of *Ding, Dong, Bell* and gave "a profound bow" when dancing *Sir Roger de Coverley* for visitors. It was here that he was first noted to be "always drawing" which resulted in his mother giving him some drawing lessons. By four years of age he was "...never so happy as when lying at full length on the floor and drawing figures of soldiers in every conceivable attitude". Many of these drawings started to be collected into scrap books at this time. His father noted that:

Toy soldier

> He learns little and cries oft but never tires of drawing his soldiers, funny little figures full of action and all his own, for he disdains the idea of copying anything.

It was the emotional contradictions of Ted's constitution, however, that most exercised his parents during this period. Both of them thought him "a queer little character". In part, perhaps, this was due to the difficulties of life in the nursery. Life was not always easy during the Victorian era, even for the upper-middle classes. In 1876 Ted's younger sister, Jessie (Jessica Frances), died, giving him his first experience with death at a very early age. Yet these inherent contrasts that appeared in Ted seem to have been fired by such a passionate intensity that they went beyond the expected range of expression in small children. On the one hand he could be generous and kind, almost to a fault, with loving arms placed around his siblings or parents, followed by a big kiss. Yet at other times he was fiercely independent. He was prone to wandering off on his own "to explore" from quite a young age. At the age of five, he toddled off alone across the moor near to Borth and when found explained that he was going for a walk and would return when he felt tired. On another occasion, when visiting Aberystwyth, he got lost. A frantic search found him crying on the knee of a local cobbler just as the Town Crier was about to be summoned. Ted was also full of laughter and fun, yet prone to fits of earnestness during which no-one could make him laugh. On these occasions he would make odd and sometimes profound comments for his age. Further, whilst he was generally noted to be of a sweet temperament he frequently exploded in violent outbursts of temper. He often showed unusual bravery and maturity, yet was always ready with floods of tears. "The least thing," was said to make him cry. On one occasion, his punishment was to be dressed in his sister Polly's clothes and stood on a table. This pendulum of contrast was to be carried out of the family home and into school.

Ted started lessons in 1878 with a Governess, Miss Watson, who found him clever but boisterous. The following year he went to join his older brother, Bernard, at Glyngarth School, a purpose built Preparatory School considered to be a model of excellence by the school examiners. His father thought him "in his element" when fighting with boys from a rival school, 'the Austinites', on his way to and from school.

The family habit of taking long walks in the countryside, often of ten miles or more, soon started Ted on the lifelong habit of collecting objects which interested him. With his father as his guide these walks, in the Cotswolds that surround Cheltenham, in the nearby Malvern Hills, or on long summer holidays by the sea, started to yield a bountiful fascination with the natural world. He started by collecting fossils and butterflies, then went on to feathers but soon moved on to "anything he can lay his hands on". His drawings, however, still focused mainly on soldiers and battles - primarily inspired at this time by the Zulu War. On one ten mile walk across Minchinhampton Common, near Amberley,

Butterfly

"... the children enjoyed the fine bracing air... where their Zulu hats went careering over the plain in a high wind."

From September 1879 the countryside came slightly closer to home. His mother took on a little farm, *Sunnymede,* on the outskirts of Cheltenham, near Up Hatherley, where she could breed her poultry and practice "scientific farming", whilst the children could keep farmyard pets. Much of the produce was consumed in the household or sold in the local area, although it was never very profitable. The farm produced over 40 varieties of apples and pears, amongst other crops, which were often shown in local agricultural shows. It was not all plain sailing; on 7 July 1884 Mary Agnes lost 46 prize chickens from a coop. A policeman was called but it was soon found to be the work of a fox. Mostly, however, the farm and its produce were a source of great pleasure and pride.

It was this Gloucestershire countryside, full of birds, beasts and flowers that inspired the young boy more and more. At the age of nine he announced to his father that he was going to become a naturalist. His mother noted that he would rather have a naturalist's ramble with his father in the countryside than enjoy the games of the playground. Although good at sports, in which he often carried off prizes - even captaining the school 2nd XI - they never truly excited him. Nor did his lessons. Although he was considered a bright pupil, his reports were usually rather a disappointment; his high spirits and mischievousness dosed with a good streak of stubborn determination to be independent meant that they were often full of the word "refuses", so much so that he sometimes had to forfeit his shorter school holidays to catch up with the work, under the despairing gaze of his mother. Unusually, perhaps, for a pupil who apparently delighted in disruption, his teachers were moved to comment on his unusual honesty. They could, they said, "always trust Ted's word". Much to the relief of his parents, his crying fits and temper tantrums ceased as he entered double figures.

Soldier

During the early summer of 1883, at the age of 11, he took his first lessons in taxidermy "from White, the bird stuffer", his first subject being a Robin. At this point too, his art-work moved more and more to recording the natural world around him. Some of the last of his soldier drawings show his imaginative reconstruction of the Battle of Tel-el-Kebir (1882), where Uncle Charlie was engaged with the British army campaign against the Egyptians. Meanwhile, he was starting to show more evidence of applying himself at school. So much so, it was thought that if he was given special tuition he might be able to pass a public school scholarship. So it was that in the autumn of 1884 Ted was sent away from Cheltenham to Clifton in Bristol, to a preparatory school set up in the shadow of the famous Clifton College and run by Mr Erasmus Wilkinson. Here is where the underlying tensions of his character which had emerged during the first twelve years of his life would begin to be moulded and fused from their adverse expressions and into character strengths.

Top left :
Edward Thomas
Wilson (ETW)
Top right and bottom:
Mary Agnes Wilson

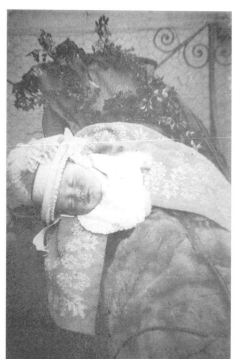

Top left: The new arrival Edward Adrian Wilson 1872
Top right: "The prettiest of my babies" Ted in 1873
Bottom left: Ted c1876 at around 4 years
Bottom right: Ted c1884 at around 12 years of age

2. "A Splendid Place for Bonnie Beasties".

Erasmus Wilkinson was a 35 year old private tutor from Marlborough. With his Yorkshire wife, Constance, his sister Mary and the help of three servants, he ran a small Preparatory School at Clifton for a dozen boy boarders. The school expected high standards from its pupils both on the academic and personal levels. It also had a higher level of tolerance for the vagaries of teenage boys - at least in so far as these were channelled into scientific exploration - than was normal for the period. As a result the schoolroom exploded with everything that the boys could find: silkworms and mice; newts and snakes; redpolls and beetles - "a regular menagerie", his father thought. It suited Ted perfectly. The schoolwork, however, came as a bit of a surprise to him, he was no longer allowed to "stare about a bit in schooltime". He wrote home to his father:

Lizard

> I have got on so far pretty well with my books, but it is hard to settle into new books after using the same for five years. I am doing my best though and shall soon get accustomed to the work.

Ted was intensely keen to do well in this new environment - so much so, that he sat with his back to his pets to concentrate fully upon his lessons. The supply of these school pets seems to have caused some consternation amongst the local populace, particularly when mixed with the Wilson family disposition for teasing and practical jokes. His future brother-in law recalled:

> ... [we] went over the downs to see him at school and true to the family traditions we took him what we knew he would love, a big tin pail of newts from Cheltenham, which we much enjoyed in the train allowing them to crawl about and horrifying the passengers who held the old belief the orange ones were poisonous.

It was in the atmosphere of his new school, which deliberately set out to foster the moral fibre of its boys, that the contrasts and deep sensitivities of Ted's highly strung character began to coalesce. Comment was made on his exceptional sense of good sportsmanship and his courteousness. This did not only extend to his fellow pupils, staff or family members. He found it increasingly difficult to accept wanton destruction in himself or others, even in the name of boyhood or science. Unusually for a collector of the Victorian era, he would never take more than one egg in four from the nest of a bird and encouraged others to follow his example. To take more from a nest became, in his eyes, mere robbery. This love of the natural world developed in him a strong sense of responsibility. On one occasion he wrote in a letter home:

> I caught a mouse by the hind legs this morning and as they were rather hurt I took it out for a walk and deposited it among some dry leaves near a house in the hope that it might find its way in.

This empathic concern, combined with his courage and independence of thought, merged with his scientific inclination during his early teens and launched him on a life-long path of struggling with Truth. He constantly wrestled throughout his life with its high ideals which he was taught at home, at school and in Church. These truths he attempted to incorporate into his own life, whether this required discipline on the scientific, artistic, moral or any other plane. It was this honest consistency at all levels of his life that was to earn the future respect of many of his fellows; but it was not attained without a great deal of hard work. Neither, however, did he ever become sanctimonious; his rich sense of humour would not allow for that. Further, the difficulties which he struggled to overcome in himself he could hardly condemn in others. Every new proposition that was presented to him was taken on merit and tested against his hard earned experience. He jettisoned those aspects which were entirely useless, merely hypocritical pietism, whether academic, ethical or religious, and incorporated that which was practical in responsible every day life. Perhaps the most remarkable thing about this process, however, was that very few people knew what was going on inside the mind of the jolly schoolboy, or later of the man. Ted was generally self effacing and was happy to simply do his best whilst staying in the background. This was deeply reminiscent of some of his illustrious Quaker ancestors. His Great Uncle, Thomas Wilson, had devoted his life to science, was a mainstay of the Philadelphia Academy of Natural Sciences and founded the Entomological Society of that city. Despite giving 28,000 specimens, 11,000 books and £5,000 to the Academy, when he found he was to be publicly thanked for his donations, he instructed them to desist or they would receive no further gifts. Whilst Ted was at Wilkinson's school, this process of struggling with truth was still emerging within him. It found expression in one way through his increasing scientific accuracy - his father was greatly impressed that Ted's beetle collection now had the males and females appropriately labelled - and in another way in the pleasure which Ted took in living on less pocket money than his parents allowed.

One of the most important changes that occurred at home during Ted's time at Clifton was his parents' decision not to renew the lease on the farm at *Sunnymede,* which they gave up in September 1885. They decided, instead, to lease a new farm, *The Crippetts,* which was situated about three statute miles (4.8 kilometres) outside Cheltenham, where Mary Agnes could indulge her new interest in Dexter Cattle. The farm was balanced on the edge of the Cotswolds on a long spur of Leckhampton Hill, near the village of Shurdington. The unusual name of 'Crippetts' is thought to derive from 'Cropet' or 'Crupet', a common Middle-English surname in Gloucestershire during the 13th century. The Tudor farm cottage stood on a site that had been occupied and farmed for many hundreds of years, employing in the region of ten people at this time, although the Bailiff was soon replaced due to his drunken inclinations. The lease was no light undertaking, costing £230 per year (equivalent to £16,000 today). More importantly, from Ted's point of view, its woods, fields and hedgerows were teeming with wildlife of every sort: badgers and foxes, red squirrels and rabbits, grass snakes, newts, birds and insects in profusion. Particular comment was made on the wonderful number of butterflies which abounded on the estate. Ted fell in love with it instantly. The pond was quickly cleared to encourage newts and frogs, a task that needed irregular attention. On one such occasion Ted was nearly drowned when he became entangled in the pond-weed but was saved by his older brother, Bernard. Ted looked forward to spending his school holidays at *The Crippetts* immensely. His father, amongst other things, was gratified that his sons would be able to "get into country habits", riding, shooting and dabbling in estate management.

Back at Clifton, in between his lessons, he continued upon his chosen path towards becoming a naturalist. He invested a sovereign in skinning and stuffing tools and used to practice on dead specimens of Mr Wilkinson's poultry. His academic work was improving but he still, at this time, made "hideous blunders", as he put it. He did not enjoy being made to play cricket (he was usually stranded at long-off) but enjoyed some other sports. He took prizes for his art work. It is said that he even gave one such prize away to another boy who had no prize and to whom it meant more.

At the age of fourteen, in 1886, he tried for public school scholarships at Charterhouse and at Marlborough but failed. In part, his classics simply were not good enough and in part he had proved so nervous at the interview that he had hardly been able to speak. Ted thought that things would have been very different if he had been sent to Wilkinson's school at the age of seven. He certainly never regretted going:

Wren

I failed to get a scholarship but learned a first-class morality. From the year 1884 when I went to Wilkinson's School at Clifton I have had an increasing disgust for impure talk, impurity in every shape, - a thing for which I shall always be grateful to that wonderfully high-toned school. I never heard a dirty word or a doubtful tale or jest there, and when I came into the thick of it afterwards I never had any share in it.

August of 1886 was spent by the entire family at *The Crippetts*. Here they "...revelled in the fine bracing air and thorough country life. Ted, home from Clifton, was busy with his gun..." It was decided that his education would be continued by sending him to Cheltenham College from the beginning of the autumn term. His Uncle Charlie was an 'Old Cheltonian' and his father was, amongst many other roles in Cheltenham, the school physician. The College was also convenient to *Westal*, so that Ted could be a day pupil rather than a boarder.

Cows

The Cheltenham Proprietary College for Boys had opened in 1841, the first public school to open during the reign of Queen Victoria. It aimed to educate the sons of gentlemen on Church of England principles and prepare them for careers in the professions or the army. One of its founders had been the Rev. Francis Close, a leading Evangelical preacher, who had helped to put Cheltenham on the map as a town where one might not only take the waters of the spa but also receive spiritual enlightenment; a fact referred to in George Eliot's novel *Middlemarch* (1872). It was also a school with interest in the moral fibre of its pupils, although perhaps not quite so enthusiastic about large numbers of pets in the classroom. This was more than made up for in Ted's mind by the fact that, as a day pupil, he wasn't tied to the school grounds at each end of the day and could wander off to *The Crippetts* to ramble in the hedgerows and observe the wildlife there. He was described as being at this time:

> ...a thin, lithe schoolboy, with close-cut, wavy, dark-red hair, a pair of unusually bright blue eyes, and a half-amused, half-quizzical expression, often turning to a merry smile...

and he could be seen hurrying down the corridors of the school at the end of the day like any other boy of his age.

This isn't to say that he didn't enjoy life at the College to the full. He was always proud of his school and valued his time there. Ted would be remembered by his fellow pupils for his kindness, helping them in the laboratories and lending his notes. His academic work was mostly solid but never outstanding. One of the masters, Mr J. Hitchins, nevertheless seems to have taken a particular interest in him and "obliged him to work to the limit of his capabilities". He played in the Day Boy XV and in their 2nd football XI. He also took up rowing whilst at the College, rowing in the 1st Day Boy IV. But he was most active in the Natural History Society, being Secretary of the ornithological section for some time. In this role one of the master's recalled that he was:

> ...most conscientious, and faced much unpopularity by correcting certain irregularities which had grown up in the collection of birds' eggs... He had even then a kind of scientific reserve which prevented him from forming conclusions without long search and observation. There was an indescribable charm about him.

Little Owl

Ted won the school prize for drawing four years in succession, geology twice, the prize for the best insect collection on more than one occasion, and in his final year, the prize for the best collection of birds' eggs. The lists of the observations made by Ted and others in the Natural History Society record the breeding cycles and migrant arrival dates for many species, some of which no longer occur with regularity around Cheltenham, from the Red-backed Shrike and Corncrake to the Cirl Bunting and Marsh Warbler. On one occasion Ted even found the nest of a Hawfinch at *The Crippetts,* a triumph long remembered in the Natural History Society at Cheltenham College, even after he had long gone. On another occasion, Ted noted a Golden Eagle that was shot at Prestbury. Such were the details of his notes that his father often used to draw upon them when preparing his lectures to give before the Cheltenham Natural Science Society.

One of the more interesting events to have occurred at the College whilst Ted was there, at least as regards subsequent history, was discussion in *The Times* about making physical education a more compulsory part of the school curriculum. At

Cheltenham College this was reflected in a meeting of the College Debating Society the motion being "That games ought to be made compulsory". Ted, who enjoyed some sports but thought that others were a terrible waste of time, was one of the two speakers against the motion; the motion was carried. Ted, however, was always pleased that he had mostly escaped the shackles of compulsory games. It was a deeply held view of his that was ultimately to shape the future of the 20th century conservation movement .

There is little doubt that whilst he enjoyed his school life much of his education was occurring outside it, in the freedom of after school hours and holidays. Indeed, his schoolwork probably suffered at times from the concentration on his natural history observations and collections. The influence of his father on this process from an early age should not, in all probability, be under-estimated. Ted was never an acquisitive person (his 'Christmas wishes' list for 1885 lists only "Books on birds, drawing materials, India ink and cheese paper", for example) but when he did want something he pressed it with vigour. He had set his heart on acquiring 'the Bee Closet', a small study-type room with plenty of shelving at *Westal*, in which his father had once kept bees. He wanted to keep his Natural History collections and pets in there. It was finally given to him for Christmas in 1886, with a set of dissecting instruments. It was a long-standing family tradition to write short verses to go with each Christmas gift. His father's poem on the gift tag of these presents seems to be quite revealing as regards his aspirations for his son and what he was trying to teach him:

A doctor in embryo here I spy
It's easy to spot him with half an eye,
For his fingers are itching to wield the knife
Which with time and patience may save a life.
Young Sir, I am sure you're athirst for knowledge
That's never dreamed of at Cheltenham College
You long, for instance, to carve a cat,
At a toad or a mouse or a full grown rat;
The inside works of every creature
Are for you the most absorbing feature;
Then study them deeply, inside and out
There's nothing that's not worth learning about.
Read, mark and digest each habit and look
Note them in brain and note them in book;
But be cautious how you draw conclusions
Or you may be landed in delusions.
I bring you the tools of your Art, my boy,
Use them wisely without annoy
To bird, beast, fish or living creature
and you'll find Dame Nature a loving teacher.

This process of being taught to observe from Nature itself - that is, not to see what you wish to see but to truly see what is present and to accurately record it - was encouraged in Ted by his father in several ways. One of the most unusual was a method that had been used in the training of ETW himself, and that of his 0brothers, by their father - and may well have been used in the family prior to this. Ted was sent out with a small amount of money for an excursion on foot

Cocklewomen at Kidwelly

with the conditions that he was to make it last as long as possible, would receive no more financing and was to bring back full notes and accounts of all that was seen and done. Ted explored most of Wales on foot over several summers, returning with numerous sketches and notes on subjects from wildlife to architecture. He was later to say that this training had taught him more of lasting value than anything else.

His powers of observation were more than amply demonstrated on 21 June 1887, the day of celebration for Queen Victoria's Golden Jubilee. The entire family went to *The Crippetts* to watch the lighting of the celebratory beacons. In the perfectly clear conditions Ted spotted a remarkable 90 bonfires along the length of the Severn Valley, from Leckhampton Hill to the Wrekin. With his powerful observational skills arose the ability to mimic - from bird calls and animal habits through to having a talent for acting. When the children started putting on short plays and other theatricals for the enjoyment of adult family members and their guests, Ted was noted to have a flair for acting his parts.

It was nevertheless at *The Crippetts* where he truly engaged these skills, training himself to be a quite remarkable field naturalist, even from this young age. He would frequently rise early in the morning, leaving the house before daybreak to be in place to observe a coppice at *The Crippetts,* or Crickley Hill. Here, wrapped in his cloak against the cold of dawn, he would watch and note the forms of the emerging light, the calls of the birds, the state of the weather, the scuttles of mice, the seasons of the wild flowers, and the arts of the fox. Often, he would return to *The Crippetts* again in the evening. One of his favourite pastimes was to buy his supper for sixpence and take it to the farm where he would sit and observe the rabbits whilst he ate it. In all seasons, but particularly in the long days of summer, he came to know every bird, plant and beast, its rituals, and its habits. *The Crippetts* was indeed "a splendid place for Bonnie Beasties" and he came to know and love them all.

The final expansion of the Wilson family occurred in 1889 with the arrival of another daughter. Gwladys Elizabeth took the total number of children to ten, although following the early death of Jessie, it was never higher than nine at any one time. Gwladys became a firm favourite with the whole family but particularly with Ted; not that he was to be living at *Westal* full time for much longer.

During 1890, in the Oxford and Cambridge exams, despite years of mixed school reports and 'must try harders', Ted obtained his certificate with honours in science. He applied to go to Gonville and Caius College, Cambridge, where he failed to obtain a full scholarship but was soon awarded status as an Exhibitioner. Ted never forgot his old school. He was to maintain close friendships with many of the pupils and masters from Cheltenham College throughout his life.

Dwarf Spurge

Top left: Ted c1888 aged about 15, "A thin lithe schoolboy with close cut wavy dark red hair"

Top right: "Popping the Question" 1889 Ted played Mr Henry Thornton L-R: Lilly; Nellie; Polly; Ted; Sybil Ker; Centre front: Bernard

Bottom right: Ted "Off to Cambridge" 1891 Standing in the French Windows at Westal

Top left:
The Wilson family, 9 surviving children in all, completed with the arrival of Gwladys in 1890
Left to Right:
Back Row: Polly; Lilly; Ted;
Middle Row: ETW; Mary Agnes with Gwladys, Nellie;
Front Row: Elsie; Jim; Ida; Bernard (with Minnie)

Bottom:
Haymaking at the Crippetts c1890
"During the summer [Ted] was busy bird-nesting, collecting and hay-making at all odd moments."

3. "Noisy Amongst the Noisiest!"

*****

Each child of God, each one of us,
has a separate part to play in upholding
the perfection of God's Wisdom,
and of bringing it to perfection in ourselves;
some by fasting and an ascetic life,
some by a convivial and social life.

EAW

*****

College life

In October 1891 Ted went up to Gonville and Caius College, Cambridge, as part of an intake of freshmen that quickly developed a reputation for being boisterous and turbulent. Many of the Cambridge Colleges were much smaller in those days than they are today and Caius was no exception; most people lived in College, so everybody knew everybody else. Ted made his mark with his peers in a typical fashion. After their first hall together many of the freshmen took coffee and sought to impress each other, boasting of their prowess as young men. One of his contemporaries recalled that:

He was silent during our discussion, until he was pointedly asked what he proposed to do. It was his first trial as a man, and he replied that he intended to work seven hours a day and also row, a position he maintained all his years in Cambridge. That night he made his mark in his year; he showed he had a character...

The fact that this event was remembered many years later meant that in his own quiet way, he must have made an impression indeed.

Ted was good to his word. He took up rowing for his College with considerable energy, writing home, "...you can't think how delightful it is to get a three or four miles row every day of the term, barring Sundays." For Ted the delight rested in the mental and physical demands of rowing which he found to be worthwhile lessons in self discipline, "...there's a fascination about keeping oneself at the treadmill...", he wrote. His pleasure when the hard work paid off was immense, he obtained his colours in the 'Lents' and the 'Mays' over subsequent years along with several pewters. This combination of self discipline, the thrill of the race and the enthusiasm with which he defended the honour of his College made rowing an undertaking which he relished.

Ted also made his mark in College by being continually in the thick of the high spirited pranks of his year. In this regard, he was a typical undergraduate. For most of his undergraduate days he was, according to a peer,

> ...an irresponsible boy... always respecting himself, but always in the midst of whatever fun and jollity that might be going, noisy amongst the noisiest...

fencing

On returning to Cambridge in 1892 after Christmas at home, he settled in rooms high up over the Gate of Virtue and Wisdom, which he was to occupy for all of his remaining days at Caius. His popularity was such that his nickname of 'Ginger' was said to be trumpeted from the courtyard below his windows with great regularity; a fact which drew comment from the Master. Being in the thick of the action also often meant sustaining physical injury:

> We all meet in a room after Hall, clear the furniture, and begin with a big jug of beer on the table and a host of tumblers. We have single sticks and fight in masks, and then every two or three minutes you receive or give a whack which doesn't disappear for a week, and as we have this every Friday you see we're always piebald.... There are about 10 or 12 of us who meet and box and fence in turns.

Ted possessed what his friend, John Fraser, later described as "...that certain passport to the College's heart - a vein of delightful humour." This sense of humour was put to good use on some occasions, particularly when the gentlemanly codes of the period were rigidly applied to these excitable young men. Ted was quite astonished at being proctorised for wearing a straw hat after dark only a few yards from the College gates. On another occasion he even managed to get sent down.

In a pool at the edge of the mill race near to Granchester Mill there lived a large and famed trout which many had tried to catch and miserably failed. Ted was a keen fisherman and combining this with his naturalist's instincts, he decided that the most likely time of day to catch it would be in the very early morning. He slipped out of College at 3 a.m., almost certainly let out by the Head Porter, Beckley, who, it is said, would have done anything for him. Ted caught the trout which he then sent to the Master as a gift. The Master was delighted and sent for Ted to enquire as to its method of capture. When Ted told him the story the Master was duly impressed and then enquired as to whether Ted had leave to go out of the College at such an hour. In those days the rules surrounding the comings and goings of students in the College were strictly regulated by a curfew. Ted admitted that he did not have leave and the Master, a strict disciplinarian, sent him down for the last few days of term, despite appeals for leniency by the Senior Tutor. This story is brilliantly illustrative of the high codes of honour which were the expected standards for gentlemanly behaviour in Victorian England.

Ted was the strictest adherent to many of these codes, yet he tried to follow them to their fullest extent rather than merely bathing in conventionality. At Cambridge he was honest, almost to the point of brutality. He rarely, at this time, held his tongue. In his own struggle towards personal integrity he was quick to criticise inconsistencies in others and could be caustic and cynical. It was not other people's viewpoints that riled him, nor even their failings. He was noted for his unusual tolerance of other people's views and foibles, even if they conflicted with his own, but he only truly respected others if they were consistent and sincere. It was lack of sincerity that would draw from him a withering comment or a contemptuous look. He particularly detested hypocrisy, self-pity and injustice. He struggled for many years to curb his tongue when he realised that the high standards of honest consistency that he expected from himself were not necessarily expected by others of themselves.

Ada and Longun studying in the Backs

If it was Ted's sense of humour that led his peers to love Ted's company, it was this straightforwardness that earned him their respect, even if they didn't always enjoy listening to what he had to say. They turned to him for advice and so he became the mediator for many of the disputes in the College. On one such occasion, one of Ted's friends was taken to have insulted a group of his acquaintances; Ted, who was already becoming noted for his loyalty to his friends, set out to mediate. On this occasion, however, his efforts were fruitless. After reasoning with a room full of the aggrieved and failing to persuade them to make up with his close friend, he announced to them that, under the circumstances, he would no longer be able to know them, and departed. Their natural indignance was followed by a plan to visit Ted one by one and tell him what they thought of him. One by one the following evening they went round to his rooms. Ted was, as intended, extremely embarrassed but, true to protocol, maintained traditional hospitality, shaking hands with them as they arrived as if it was a formal call. By the end of the evening, all of the visitors had been so impressed by him that they ended up as better friends than before, all agreeing to drop any active retaliation on his close friend. It was this moral power of Ted's character which John Fraser later recalled:

He was essentially a very just, tolerant, and extra-ordinarily strong man. He was utterly fearless and would condemn a man's action which was not pure and sound in the strongest possible way.

A measure of the esteem in which Ted came to be held by his peers was his election to the 'Shakespearian Society', a very exclusive club for the leading sportsmen of the time, amongst whose ranks Ted could not truly be said to have numbered, sportsman though he was. In addition to rowing he played for the second rugby team and carried off the University prize for diving in his final year. His diving led to an accident where he hit a brick on the bottom of the river whilst practising and received substantial lacerations to his face and chest. He was also active in two College literary societies, the 'Fortnightly' and 'Science and Art', taking regular part in discussions and reading occasional papers. He even served as Secretary to the Fortnightly Society in the Lent term of 1893. He was a strong supporter of the Caius Mission. Five men of his year also started 'intellectual Sunday evenings' from 8-12 p.m. where they would sit in someone's rooms, smoke and drink coffee whilst listening to classical music, which they discussed, along with art and poetry. It was during this period that Ted fell in love with the works of Tennyson, reading him with great regularity throughout his life.

All these activities, of course, took place against a background of solid work. Ted kept to the schedule which he had outlined for himself on his first night. He seems to have made solid progress, as his Exhibition was continued and he became life-long friends with several of the masters. His interests in the natural world did not fade, however. He regularly took long walks collecting specimens and making notes on all the wildlife to be found in the Cambridge area - so much so that his friends thought that his rooms were a regular museum. As an artist too, he made remarkable progress during his Cambridge years. In part, his development came from working and re-working his pictures. He started to perfect his own system of colour notation, writing on his pencil sketches the colours which he was seeing and perfecting it as a form of shorthand. He developed this system into a remarkable form of colour memorisation, so that he could reproduce the exact shade in paint several months later. Progress was also due to the atmosphere amongst his peers where it was quite acceptable to read about artists and then discuss their merits. He would often amuse such visitors to his rooms by doing their silhouette and soon amassed a substantial collection of portraits. He also undertook some travel in Europe with friends during the holidays, where he was exposed to many great works. During the summer of 1892 he matriculated at the University of Göttingen with his friend Young. They travelled via Rotterdam, Antwerp, Brussels, Cologne and Cassel, visiting many of the major sites and art galleries along the way. He made extensive notes on various artists, with the sights that he saw, including the duels which he witnessed amongst the students in Göttingen, duelling still being a part of the Gentleman's code in Germany at the time. He also climbed a tree and obtained a young Red Kite which he brought home to Cheltenham and named 'Milan'. It was a very troublesome pet, and

Sihouette of Jabez Charles

caused some consternation to his parents. It was finally sent to the London Zoo in 1896. In the Easter break of 1894 he went with a large reading party to Blankenberge in Belgium from where he visited Bruges and Antwerp. These visits, combined with visits at home to the great Cathedrals and the London galleries led him to write home that he was "...working up a lunacy for pictures and poesie." What had particularly excited him was the realisation that even the great artists had had to learn their technique. In the absence of time for formal art lessons, he therefore studied their works to develop his own skills.

Underneath the surface of work, sport, revelry and general popularity, however, Ted remained a very shy, highly strung and private man. He was noted by his contemporaries as being a man with very many acquaintances and only a few, very close friendships. Few people were ever privileged to know his deep inner thoughts, the level on which his struggling with Truth occurred. Those who did were influenced by him for life. On a simple level, many of his private thoughts were perfectly ordinary. As a freshman, for example, his worries were similar to those of freshmen today: practical concerns connected with being away from home and responsible for one's self for the first time. He wrote home to find how much he should be paying for tea or to re-sole his boots, since he did not want to be over-charged. Yet this also connects through to the deeper levels of Ted's character. Frugality was always something which Ted practised in his life; he always tried to make do on less than his privileged position in Society allowed him. Some, especially at Cambridge, mistook this for poverty, which strictly speaking, it was not - his father was prepared to give him whatever money he asked for - it was a moral choice about materialism. Superficially, these deeper processes also showed themselves through the fact that although Ted was always in the thick of things he almost never drank to excess, or the fact that it was well known in College that he wasn't to be asked to heavy meals as he didn't appreciate them - many thought because he couldn't afford to reciprocate. Few guessed at the deeper thinking that lay behind what, for the times, was a simple life. It was at Cambridge that much of his thinking and wrestling with Truth started to distil in Ted's mind and set the scene for the practice of moral Truth within his own life. This Truth had by now become firmly embodied for him in Biblical Truth, as expressed through the life of Christ. He had always been Christian in slightly more than the nominal sense. When he had been confirmed at the age of 18, he wasn't very sure that the good Bishop of Gloucester had achieved very much as he already felt very much a "child of God", particularly when walking out in the wilds of the Cotswolds. But it was at Cambridge that he really started to engage with the moral demands made on the life of each individual by the New Testament - to make it his own, as it were. Widespread theological discussions with his friends doubtless helped him to focus his views. His reading of Thomas à Kempis, sparked a letter to his sister in November 1893, which summarised his thinking at this time:

> Well, Pol, you've spotted what I was going to write about last week as to the selfish tone in Thomas à Kempis. I spoke about it to a man up here and we decided that it is one of the failings of an ascetic's life such as a monks. His whole idea is to get the peace of mind which comes with self restraint and self abasement. Well we decided that that is only one of the first steps towards a really higher life. Well you see I can't take that step yet, as I've told you. But I've decided that if I once got hold of that perfect self control, then a higher ideal than a monk's life would be open to one, namely to let your own soul go to the devil, as far as you could see, if it could in any way by doing so help others. By going to the devil I don't mean it literally but merely that you might get into a state so much wrapped up in the welfare of others that your own never crossed your mind; this is where I think a monk's life failed that in all cases except such as those of the highest saints we read of, they sat down for a lifetime to take the first step, namely to get self control. N'est ce pas? Well, I think <u>that</u> could be got with a good will in a much shorter time, it ought to be got in the ordinary run of events though I must say I think that an ascetic's life would be <u>much</u> more conducive to it, since it has so many temptations removed. I naturally really think Pol, that a monk's life, if there is such a thing to be found now, would make a person of the present state of society sit up for the rest of his life if he went in for it for a year or so with the dogged determination to become master of himself and his feelings in every respect, and then leave it and take the regular run of life with everybody else. This is the most fascinating ideal I think I have ever imagined to become entirely careless of your own soul and body in looking after the welfare of others. But as with most things of this sort the first step is the hardest to pass.

He may not have felt able to take the first step at the end of 1893 but there seems little doubt that this was the agenda which he was setting himself for his life and subsequently set about attempting to achieve step by small step until the day he died.

During his time at Cambridge, Ted would often return to Cheltenham for the holidays. He never lost his profound love of his home area, nor of his family, continuing to possess a strong sense of duty regarding what he owed to them. As well as catching up with family, he continued his exploration and recording of the local countryside, especially around *The Crippetts*. He would often stay at the farm, sometimes alone, sometimes with family members, and frequently with friends from College for a week or two of quiet revision. Here, they enjoyed the peace and quiet of the country air, although the fields around the house were often witness to the playing of wild and crazy games such as "Robber Captain", usually in the disused quarry known as "the Allotments". At the end of one Easter vacation his father thought it would be "hazardous" to guess as to the contents of the stock pot. Ted started to execute passable watercolour landscapes. His visits were not always so pleasant, however. A large fire at *Westal* shortly before Christmas of 1893 caused the usual jollity of the occasion to be rather muted and many of the traditions were forgone, although the servants and farm hands still assembled to receive gifts in one of the undamaged rooms. It wasn't helped by the insurance investigator whom Ted's father described as an

*Student in Gown
1891 - 5*

"odious, offensive little toad who seemed to think we had set things on fire on purpose." A worse tragedy was to befall the family during the summer of 1894. During August, Gwladys, the youngest and favourite of all, died suddenly of an unknown fever. Amidst the grief Ted possessed a calmness "almost unnatural" according to his father. In a last act of remembrance he sat in her room and sketched her on her death bed. Ted and his brothers, with staff from *The Crippetts,* carried her to her resting place at Leckhampton, where many of the family were eventually to lie. The family then repaired to Nevin, in North Wales for a holiday to come to terms with their loss.

Ted's hard work at Cambridge paid off. In May 1894 he passed the first part of his MB exam and took a 1st class honours in the Natural Science Tripos Part I. For his prize he received a treasured set of five volumes of Ruskin, whose thoughts on aesthetics were deeply influential on him. His parents came to see him row for the College and it was during this visit that the Master, who thought that Ted's enormous influence on College life was of great value, expressed his wish that Ted should stay up at College for another year and do the second parts to the exams. Ted did not wish to do so:

> I am afraid, Dad, I am quite set against taking the 2nd part of the Tripos. It will not help me in the F.R.C.S. I don't want to take to scientific work for itself: I don't like it sufficiently... but what I am anxious to get on to is the practical part of Med. and Surgery. I am certain I shall do better in it than I have done in anything so far.

The majority opinion of his elders seems to have persuaded him to give it a go, however, and so he stayed on. On one level it was not a success as he failed both the MB and the Tripos and was certain that he could have passed one if he had not attempted the other. On a personal level, however, he never regretted it, it gave him an extra year to devour "pictures and poesie" before his "real work" started. This commenced in October 1895 when Ted went to take up his practical medical training at St. George's Hospital, London.

Baites Bite

Top left: Gate of Virtue and Wisdom,
Caius College, Cambridge 1892
Top right: Self Portrait c1895
Bottom: Gwladys on her death bed 1894
Inscribed: "Ye shall be sorrowful but your
sorrow shall be turned to joy"

Top: Ted's rooms at Cambridge 1894
Bottom right: Ted at Cambridge 1894
Bottom left: Life at Cambridge, Drinking in someone's rooms
L-R Ted; C.S. Myers
(Founder of the National Institute of Industrial Psychology);
John Lea (Registrar, London University); Pollard

Top left: Ted with 'Milan' his pet kite in the garden at Westal 1893
Top right: Ted 1893
Bottom: Ted diving into the river Cam, Cambridge c1895

4. "The Teaching Power of Sickness"

*****

The main thing is whether a person
has the spirit of God in him,
which to my mind means simply the
power to love and be kind and unselfish;
and many people have this in a very
perfect form without professing any religious
belief at all, or using any religious practices to keep it.
EAW

*****

Starlings

Ted took up lodgings in Westbourne Grove, London, but soon moved to a cheaper room at Delamere Crescent in Paddington. From here he would walk daily to and from his work at St. George's hospital, which in those days was located at Hyde Park Corner. He often made small detours through the parks to feast his eyes on a patch of green amidst the bricks and mortar. From 10 a.m. to 4 p.m. every day he was in the hospital and having a thoroughly good time: "It is just ripping...The teaching is perfect and in time I shall have a good shot at the F.R.C.S." He played rugby for the hospital in his spare time and was later asked to row in the hospital four-oar, which he did.

He still returned to Cheltenham to visit *Westal* and *The Crippetts* as much as he was able, his time at the farm becoming more valuable to him through constituting a break from the big city. During one such visit to *Westal* his mother suggested to him that, in his enthusiasm for medicine, he was being unsympathetic to his patients. As a result they discussed the concept of "the teaching power of sickness" over the following months, the notion that some medical conditions developed mental and spiritual fortitude whilst some did not. If it was his father who had influenced his scientific mind, it was with his mother that he had always explored theological or spiritual matters. His father refused to discuss such subjects in any depth, much to Ted's regret. Mary Agnes, however, had been brought up in the hey day of evangelical preaching in Cheltenham and was deeply religious. Ever sensitive to his own shortcomings, he replied to her after she had paid him a visit in November 1895:

> I <u>was</u> glad to see you here tho' I expect you found me unsympathetic as usual; my bowels of compassion are often - well, want pills but to complete the analogy - perhaps I feel the more. I expect my want of sympathy comes from my never having had an illness which was not my own fault... I shall get more openly compassionate as I see more illness which isn't brought about by obvious folly or sin.

This, he deliberately set out to do. On one such occasion he was heading back to London after visiting Cheltenham in May 1896. He secretly stopped off in Gloucester, where a smallpox epidemic was raging, and spent the day at the isolation fever hospital observing the disease at every stage. He walked on to Churchdown and lay on the hill to disinfect and to digest what he had seen, before continuing on his way. This challenge: to find compassion within himself for even the most unjust, hypocritical and self-pitying patient, whose illness could be described as nothing but the result of their own behaviour; to combine faith and science within the clinical practice of medicine; seems to have been one of the greatest challenges of his medical studies. With a lot of struggling, he did eventually achieve it, writing to his mother,

> ...Heaven is with us here, not in the skies to be reached only after death...Whenever we see God in another we get a glimpse of the place where He is and that is the joy of heaven.

Several of Ted's patients would eventually write of the extra-ordinary tenderness and compassion which he had exhibited to them during their treatment.

Ted also continued to work on disciplining himself as an artist. His room

> ...looked over acres of chimney-pots and a Plane tree, all of which I drew most accurately because I was reading Ruskin on truth in drawing being the main thing to aim at.

He spent hours drawing the detail of every brick. By special permission, obtained through introductions from Uncle Charlie, he also spent a part of each day drawing the animals in the Zoo; sometimes he could be found drawing in the Natural History Museum; or sometimes he would search the London parks, or amongst the stalls of the flower sellers, for mushrooms and flowers to paint. During weekends off he would spend hours with his friend, John Fraser, discussing everything from medicine and art to theology and politics. They often spent such days on Wimbledon Common, listening to the Nightjars and Nightingales. Ted thought of it as being "one of God's ditches".

Stag Beetle

It was also here in London, where for the first time Ted could be said to be truly living on his own, that he started to experiment with the practice of the ascetic ideal which he had theorised at Cambridge, restricting his own needs and wants to lose himself in the service of others. During his life at Caius College, many of his friends had thought that he lived an ascetic life - and in comparison to the average Cambridge undergraduate of the period, he did - but his experiments toward putting asceticism into practice in London were considerably more extreme. Every morning before he started the day's work he annotated and paraphrased the New Testament, completing almost the entire text during his time in London. This practice of annotated spiritual reading was continued throughout his life. He prided himself on living 'comfortably' on around 8 shillings per week - a tiny sum, even for the period - living on chestnuts or baked potatoes from street stalls and toast and watercress in his rooms. His only luxury was tobacco, of which he smoked a great deal. His clothes and shoes became worn through and probably the only thing that stopped him from being confused for a vagabond was his scrupulous cleanliness and immaculate tidiness of dress. For him, this experimentation was a way of making his faith the very essence of his life, with a priority of practical over theoretical reason, "Deeds, not Words" as the Wilson family motto bluntly declares. Or as a friend of his from St. George's phrased it:

> For Wilson religion was a divine life, not a divine science; and embodied personalities and examples not philosophical systems or doctrinal formulas. He sought and cared little for originality, but greatly and entirely for truth.

Again, however, if you had ever met him, you would never have known, unless you became one of the very few people in whom he confided. He never saw the point in expressing his views to someone else, unless they asked. A quiet, shy man with great courtesy; a ripping sense of humour but a gentle manner; ginger hair and bright blue eyes; a long, slightly stooping stride; and an ever ready smile, matched only by his readiness to do whatever he could to help: these are the characteristics that most of his acquaintances remembered. He would draw sketches of the staff and his fellow students during lectures, much to their delight, and freely lent his notes and experience, just as he had at Cambridge or at Cheltenham College. His popularity at St. George's was illustrated through his being the only 'dresser' invited to the nurse's concert, a privilege which greatly pleased him.

Brown Rats

The Wilson family was again subjected to the trauma of untimely death in March 1896, when Ted's older sister Nellie (Helen Edith), who was a nurse at the Leicester Royal Infirmary, died in the line of duty. She contracted and died of Enteric fever (Typhoid) during an epidemic. Quite what Ted made of this incident is unclear; it was certainly a reminder of the daily risks to the lives of medical personnel during this period, but it was also a deep shock to a close knit family. This should, perhaps, have served as a warning to him when Dr Rolleston, under whom he was working at the time, sent him back to *Westal* for a week in October 1896 because his health appeared so run down; but it did not. Ted thought that all that he needed was "a decent atmosphere for a bit", some time out of the thick smogs and pea-soup pollution of industrial London; even in these he managed to appreciate beauty, noting the startling colours of the unusual London sunsets which the thick smoke caused.

Not long after his return to London, he moved his residence to Battersea where he lived at the Caius Mission with the Warden and his wife, the Leighton-Hopkins. Here he had to "put up with a little Society every day" which he thought would do him good, since he immensely disliked the hypocrisy of 'Society'. It may have been 'Society' behind the front door but the Mission was in the centre of the Battersea slums. Here the educated classes of Victorian England strove to better the lot of the working class slum dwellers (similar to the modern practice of 'taking a year off' to go and 'do good' in the Third World). The Leighton-Hopkins looked after him as one of their own and they tried to ensure that he ate full meals. For his part, he found that living here exceeded his self-imposed budget and so what few valuables he possessed were usually in hock at the Pawn-brokers. He walked the three miles each way to the hospital, through Battersea park and along the Thames, where he enjoyed watching and noting the birds as he passed. Despite the best efforts of the Leighton-Hopkins, he often skipped dinner to go to an art gallery, to find some wildlife, or to attend a public lecture. He even went to hear the Arctic explorer Fridtjof Nansen speak. He was "smitten to distraction" by Turner's drawings - and Turner became one of the lasting influences on the development of his artistic technique, along with Ruskin and Japanese water-colourists. His midwifery course meant long hours in the slums and little sleep. Later he was 'dressing' for a surgeon whom he greatly admired. He had long respected surgeons who were able to coolly and skilfully cut somebody else up "for their own good". This meant even longer hours "yesterday I was at the hospital from 9am. to midnight, one accident after another".

On top of his hospital work and sports, his ascetic practices, his studying for his Cambridge exam re-sits and general interests in art and culture, at the Mission Ted had also started to run something similar to a modern youth club for two nights of the week; the children often being affected with eye infections, croup, adenoids, fleas, lice and eczema. He also ran the children's service on Sunday morning and spent Sunday afternoons teaching a Bible class to a group of boys, after which he would walk miles over to Paddington to hear his favourite preacher.

Swifts

Ted found teaching quite challenging but, for all the children's antics, they seem to have adored him and he them. It was perhaps this which inspired him to think about taking up missionary work in Africa, an idea which he agreed to postpone in the face of parental opposition, at least until he had qualified. This may also be seen as indicative of the fact that he was increasingly depressed, restless and ill at ease in London. "Springtime" he wrote, "and yet in London I feel like a soda water bottle in an oven". To his mother, he sent an equivocal assurance:

> Mother may rest assured that I am as fit as a doe. Only too abominably fit to live in this damned overtrodden cock and hen yard with any comfort to my soul. The fitter I feel the more I swear.

If Ted thought that he was doing too much, his deep sense of honour and loyalty meant that he was not prepared to let anyone down. He wrote to his mother,

> One must not throw over responsibilities which one has undertaken, that's a certainty. If one finds one has made a mistake one must live it through, even if it is life-long. Maybe it is the Cross one has to bear day by day for Christ's sake. I am quite convinced that everyone should follow his own conscience so long as it does not interfere with any responsibility previously undertaken. If we find it does, we have made an error and we must just take the consequences.

Ted continued to take on more work, becoming an ex-officio member of the Church Council and doing occasional preaching. He gave up alcohol for a while, in order that he wouldn't be a hypocrite when trying to help alcoholics in the slums and thought of taking up boxing again after his brief flirtation with it at Cambridge. He joined the Graphic Society at St. George's. In the hospital, his artistic talent had, by now, been noticed. Several leading doctors had started to use his skills in pathological drawing. Dr Rolleston even asked Ted to illustrate his book on *Diseases of the Liver* (1905), whilst another friend asked him to part illustrate a book on Fishing Flies, *Old Flies in New Dresses* (1898). Ted watched Queen Victoria ride through the streets in procession for her Diamond Jubilee and made sketches of her in her carriage, spending a full day walking the processional routes and watching the illuminations in the evening. He took a trip to France with his friend Charles and fell in love with Rouen.

Chrysanthemums

All, however, was not well. New Years Day 1898 was memorable to Ted because he started to read for the first time the *Life of St. Francis of Assisi*, who epitomised for him everything that he had come to believe for himself. For his parents, however, it was a time of great anxiety: Ted was clearly unwell. He returned to his gruelling schedule in London, increased even further by the fact that he was deputising for the Mission Warden whilst he was away. By March, he also accepted the fact that something was not quite right and went to consult Dr Rolleston. After tests, he was informed that he had developed Pulmonary Tuberculosis and should seek treatment at once. His friends Charles and Fraser came around to pack his things for him and he was shipped off home to *Westal*, protesting that he was merely "soot sodden".

He was put to bed upon his arrival home with strict orders to rest. After a week he was up and about at *The Crippetts* but was at *Westal* on 12 March when a formal visit was paid by Miss Oriana Souper. Ted had first met her at the Caius Mission where she had been a house guest of the Leighton-Hopkins for a few days. He had secretly stolen down the stairs again one evening, after he had retired, to listen to her sing and had passed another blissful evening alone in her company talking by the fire until late, a fact which greatly surprised their hosts when they returned home. Although obviously greatly smitten, he had said nothing, preferring to wrestle with these new feelings in private. Since that visit, several months earlier, she had, quite by coincidence, taken a post as 'matron' at St. James' School in Cheltenham. The Leighton-Hopkins had therefore put them back in touch and she came to call upon *Westal*.

Not that Ted would have thought that this mattered very much, pleasurable though it was. A diagnosis of Pulmonary Tuberculosis was, in those days, usually a death sentence. There was no treatment beyond getting plenty of rest and fresh air. There seems little doubt that, once the gravity of the diagnosis had been digested, everybody, including Ted himself, expected the outcome to be death.

Delamere Crescent, Paddington,
"there was.. a corner of brickwork
in front ... and I copied each brick."
September 1896

5. "Eternal Heaven"

Ted trusted his fate, as he always did, into the hands of God. He went to stay at *The Crippetts,* the place that he loved best in all the world, calling it "a little piece of heaven". It was where he would have chosen to die. His friend, John Fraser later recalled that "To see Wilson at his best one had to go and stay with him at *The Crippetts*. There he was really at home and in his natural place." At *The Crippetts* Ted busied himself breathing in the country air and drawing and painting the world around him with a remarkable intensity. For him there was by now - if there ever had been - no division between science and faith, since science was a way of getting to know God's creation more intimately. Nor was there a division between faith and art, since art was a form of rejoicing in God's world, learning to see it in new ways. Painting and drawing were, for him, a form of prayer. Science and faith, health and sickness, art and prayer, death and life itself, in all its rich manifestations, were, for Ted, all different forms of exploring one indivisible divine Truth. It was for this reason that he immensely disliked selling his pictures, although he very occasionally did so, writing at this time that it was "rather like selling a little bit of yourself which isn't even your own to sell."

Rabbits

If the intensity of his painting at this time can therefore be seen as prayer under difficult circumstances, as rejoicing in the world whilst he still could, then it should be understood that it was not something about which he was moribund. The pictures are vibrant and alive. He wrote later that the thought that death was within measurable distance had brought him great peace of mind. He was also busy interspersing his thoughts with typical, humorous skits. He wrote to his sister Polly at the end of April:

> Why haven't you written to me? Every milk cart a new disappointment. I have so wanted a word or two of news. I have said to myself "Possess ye your blooming soul in patience", also "I won't write till I hear from her". But good gracious me,

I want to know if Mary is well, that's about all. You might ask her or anyone else after her, if she wants a squirrel full of fleas, quite tame, quite strong, and nearly domesticated. He feeds himself on anything you give him, and so on. He ate a hole in my sheet and made a nest of the bits. Little beast. Loads of fleas, ever fresh and ever young ones, all sizes. Ask her if she'll have them, if you think fit and have the chance. I leave it to you... Time for sketching Pol, you had better come home soon, we will do some this month. I have only done black and white so far, except flowers, newts, beasts and devils. Once or twice I have seen heaven. I painted a primrose there. I have also got a snake. It has no fleas. I will send it with the squirrel, if they will have him... Upon my soul, the glory of God in Nature has never been so continually before me as it is now. And no-one to tell of it. Sometimes I feel full to overflowing with it.

His sister Polly actually spent a great deal of time at *The Crippetts* with Ted and 'Pugie' the Red Squirrel, bird-nesting, botanising, sketching and laughing. They were frequently joined by "the useful help", Miss Souper. Ted was immensely happy.

Mosquito

Hungry. An unexpected introduction through some family friends resulted in an invitation to spend the summer with Mr and Mrs Rice at their farmhouse, *Hårstad,* in Terråk, near to modern day Brønnøysund, in the southern part of northern Norway. It was felt that the vast expanses of fresh air would do him good and so Dr Rolleston approved the trip. He left England at the end of May, soon experiencing a new kind of liberty: "no-one is ever waited on at any meal, and things are Not Hungry - not kept hot for one." He found it refreshing: "I never realised such freedom", he wrote. He used it to full advantage, roaming vast areas of wilderness at will, tramping through the forests and moors of northern Norway on his first visit to the sub-polar regions. He found walking in this area quite challenging because of the rapacious clouds of mosquitoes and horse flies, which "were so thick on my leg that you couldn't see any stocking." His fingers and legs were bitten and swollen "like German sausages". The self-control which he had accomplished through his ascetic practise by this point in his life, is perhaps best illustrated by the fact that he had the patience to sit and draw the mosquitoes whilst they bit him. "Their bites are funny to watch. If you let them suck their fill and leave them of their own accord there is no bump raised and no irritation." He was most keen to find a Goshawk nest but just as excited to find the nests of Brambling, Fieldfare and Capercaillie. The woods were so vast, however, that he felt rather lost trying to find birds nests in them at all and often sat to paint flowers. On one occasion during his walks he came across a large herd of reindeer and a small Lapp village which he explored with interest. But it was the vibrant colours of the northern landscape streaked by a never quite darkened sun, the long pseudo-nights of merged sunrises and sunsets in which effusions of yellow, red and purple light fired the forests and snowy mountains in skeins of shifting colours, that truly took his breath away. "It takes a lot of yellow paint and tobacco but the results are remarkable", he wrote home. As the mosquitoes filled themselves upon him, so he in turn filled sketch books with paintings to show his family. Despite the excitement, however, he was not well and missed home, particularly *The Crippetts*. He thought that the ideal solution might be to bring the two together.

> If one could plant The Crippetts up here as far as this is from towns and conventions and night, and shift the mosquitoes, I wouldn't grumble at it for an eternal heaven.

Mr Rice was so impressed with the way that Ted had treated the illness of one of their other guests that he wanted Ted to stay as a medical advisor. In August, however, he returned to England as planned, where he managed to spend most of his time at his beloved *Crippetts* with his family and Miss Souper, rambling the hedgerows and telling tales of the wild north. Mostly, he sketched. From here he often walked to Gloucester, making detailed sketches of the Cathedral, whose earthy Romanesque elegance inspired him. It was his favourite piece of architecture. He also often walked to Tewkesbury, sketching the town and the Abbey. There was an overgrown canal in the town which was one of his favourite natural history haunts. At the end of August, however, he had a feverish attack: the tuberculosis had not gone away. It was decided in consultation with Dr Rolleston, therefore, that he should be sent to Davos in Switzerland for a winter of treatment in a sanatorium.

He left for Davos in October, travelling via the south of France and Zurich. He fell in love with the vibrant colours of the south of France but as he headed into the Alps his mood responded to the dullness of the weather. These days the town of Davos is full of tourists going skiing. At the end of the nineteenth century skiing was relatively unheard of; Davos was a major European centre for treating tuberculosis, its comparatively dry air supposedly aiding the cure of the disease. Ted loathed it: "...oh, the ugliness of Davos Platz and Dorf, all pensions and hotels, all cold and white and ghastly." He was extremely unhappy. He was confined to his elegant hotel quarters by his doctor and told to eat large quantities of food. Ted changed his hotel to save money and continued his Spartan existence, although he stopped smoking for several months at Davos, at his mother's specific request. Neither the doctors nor his fellow patients much inspired him to begin with:

> The conversation at meals is all on bacilli and hearts and weights and Huggard (the doctor) and expectoration, so that one hardly dare clear one's throat because one feels as if one had said something tuberculous; still more, I think, the want of a smoke begets a desire to bite everybody and run away...

He tried hard to look upon his treatment as a penance but kicked against becoming "a cabbage" whenever he was able. He thought that his tuberculosis could not be cured and was deeply frustrated at being cooped up when there was so much of life still to be celebrated and explored. Ted eventually learned a great deal from his doctors, however, particularly the essentials of treating tuberculosis, which he decided had a great deal to do with supervision and not a lot to do with the climate. He also made some good friends amongst his fellow patients:

> I have come to feel that these five months are an equaliser. I did too much during the last two years and now I have to sit awhile. But I know there are one or two here who are happier for that very reason and that makes me as happy as anyone can wish.

Crested Tit

When he eventually persuaded the doctor to let him take "a little exercise", he went on long walks climbing high into the Alps where he watched Ptarmigan and found the tracks of a bear; he slipped and fell down a snow slope severely bruising himself and cutting his face; and when he was finally allowed to skate he spent several hours each day skating on the frozen lake. Skiing, however, still sent his temperature up and the doctor did his best to slow down Ted's activity. In some of the long hours of enforced idleness, he sat in his fireless room writing long letters home, whilst the ink froze in the bottle. His newest, and increasingly most important correspondent, was Miss Souper. He learned to sketch snow but found the grey, snowy landscape depressing. Much of his time Ted just sat and read or meditated, particularly on the life of St. Francis who had become a major inspiration to him. Some have remarked that it was at Davos that the foundations of Ted's active mysticism were laid. In fact, the foundations were created long before he came to Davos. Whilst here he certainly underwent mystic experiences, having strong premonitions, vibrant dreams and experiencing advanced meditative states. These, however, were the fruition of many years of work. Additionally, the challenge of his illness meant that Ted developed a depth of character and equanimity that comes only from the humility of facing the frustration, pain and fear of one's own death; and accepting it:

> No sorrow or sickness or parting or death or trouble of any kind is anything but a joy to anyone who has got Eternal Life in front of him, because they are all paths in the right direction and none of them can last.

With the arrival of spring, Ted seemed to find a new energy. The blooming of the alpine flowers, emergence of butterflies and return of migrant birds warmed his heart as much as the longer hours of sunlight; each new aspect was noted with delight. He wrote to Miss Souper, "I can't explain to anyone how one can so get to love a bird as to kiss every egg in its nest and to pray for them...". The period of his abstinence from smoking ended and he renewed the habit with vigour, although he gave it up again permanently within a few years. He spent a great deal of time sketching and painting, perfecting his colour notation technique, sometimes painting the same peak over and over again, working to capture the subtlety of the varying colours played onto it by the changing light of the sun. Ted started to realise that the impossible was happening to him; he was recovering - and he thought it wonderful to be alive.

In May 1899, he returned to England. His doctor thought his condition was greatly improved and recommended a quiet life, finishing his medical studies and taking up pathological drawing. Ted wasn't having any of it.

> I can't bear people who always take for granted that one's main object is to save up one's health and strength, eyesight and what not, for when one is sixty. How on earth can they tell whether one is going to reach thirty?

The family retired to *The Crippetts,* often with Miss Souper, throwing the windows of the cottage wide open, living the country life, as the English countryside reigned before them in its summer glory. They wandered through it at will, botanising and bird-nesting and enjoying being alive together. Ted was, however, unusually reserved; he had new decisions to make about his future and didn't seem to want to discuss them with anyone. He had already caused more than one raised eyebrow by coming home from Davos almost a complete vegetarian, only eating fish very occasionally. His experiences of a new found freedom were making it difficult for him to relish the prospect of fitting back in. Although he wanted to continue his medical studies, he was less sure what to do with himself when they were finished; he had become unhappy with the idea of becoming a general practitioner or an F.R.C.S. and his tuberculosis had meant that he had finally given up any idea of going to work in Africa.

His thoughts were interrupted by an invitation from the Rices to spend another summer with them in Norway, which he decided to do. By mid-June Ted was back in the northern forests, staying in a small shack far from civilisation, and revelling in the mountains, lakes and valleys of the land of the midnight sun. He would often sleep all day, then walk and sketch during the twilight at night. He made friends with a group of Lapps in the higher ranges and spent a night in their hut (saeter), where he was able to make detailed notes and sketches of them and

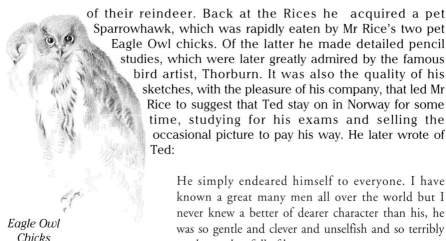

of their reindeer. Back at the Rices he acquired a pet Sparrowhawk, which was rapidly eaten by Mr Rice's two pet Eagle Owl chicks. Of the latter he made detailed pencil studies, which were later greatly admired by the famous bird artist, Thorburn. It was also the quality of his sketches, with the pleasure of his company, that led Mr Rice to suggest that Ted stay on in Norway for some time, studying for his exams and selling the occasional picture to pay his way. He later wrote of Ted:

Eagle Owl Chicks

> He simply endeared himself to everyone. I have known a great many men all over the world but I never knew a better of dearer character than his, he was so gentle and clever and unselfish and so terribly modest and so full of humour...

Mr Rice was certain that Ted could rise to be amongst the foremost bird painters and tried to do whatever he could to encourage him. Ted soon collected another pet, a young Buzzard, by descending a great cliff on a rope. Soon afterwards, however, he had an accident, seriously cutting his foot whilst walking in the woods, it became infected and it was thought better that he return home early. He was back at *Westal* by the end of August, once again a reluctant invalid, if only temporarily.

Ted, his sister Polly and Miss Souper spent some happy weeks at *The Crippetts* sketching and botanising. His pet Buzzard caused great amusement, particularly on the occasion when it landed in a plate of tomatoes during supper. It caused further chaos at *Westal* by again landing on the table. It finally ended up with 'Milan', the Red Kite, in London Zoo.

In early October, Ted returned to London to renew his interrupted medical studies. He returned to his rooms in Paddington but his feverish cough resumed with a vengeance and he was compelled to return to Cheltenham; the pollution of London was still too much for him. It appears to have finally concentrated Ted's mind on at least one aspect of his future direction, however, as on 19 October he and Miss Souper announced their engagement to be married. For ever afterwards in the family Miss Souper was known by the name of Ory, from her first name of Oriana.

Ted and Ory moved into lodgings at Stanmore, in Middlesex, close enough to London for Ted to continue his work and far enough out that he escaped the grips of its smog. He now had two months before he was due to re-sit the second part of his MB exam at Cambridge, and eighteen months work to catch up. It is was an extraordinary achievement that when he re-sat it in early December, he passed. He was now able to work upon his thesis for the degree, writing on *Yellow Atrophy of the Liver.* Ted and Ory also made the obligatory rounds of visits to relatives. In March 1900, Ted went up to Liverpool to say goodbye to his brother, Bernard, who was off to fight in the Boer War. Ted was increasingly becoming a pacifist. When news of the brutality of this conflict arrived from the front line, he found it deeply distressing.

Whilst Ted waited for his recovery to be completed, to more effectively take up medical appointments, he deliberately set out to re-train himself to paint. Despite many encouraging comments from experts, he still felt that he could not paint well. He found this particularly frustrating with birds. It was one thing, he thought, to paint a dead bird but what he actually wanted to do was to paint the life in the bird. He spent most of his time drawing and painting the abundant bird life of the nearby Stanmore Common. He started to prepare illustrations for *Land and Water* and the *Lancet.* Through his father's friend Dr Sclater (Secretary of the Zoological Society of London) who was impressed with his work, he was again granted the facility to draw at London Zoo. He was, therefore, also to be found here on a regular basis drawing the birds and other animals. Ted was further invited by Dr Sclater to a meeting of the British Ornithological Union where he enjoyed a very successful evening and was proposed as a member. He met many eminent naturalists there, including the bird artist, Lodge, who subsequently introduced him to Thorburn. They discussed his work with him and showed him some of theirs. Unbeknownst to Ted, many of the gentlemen whom he met that evening were to play an important role in his future.

'Milan' the Kite at London Zoo

In early June 1900, Ted was absolutely astonished to receive a letter from Dr Sclater informing him that the post of Junior Surgeon and Zoologist was available for the forthcoming British National Antarctic Expedition, and suggesting that he would be a suitable applicant. Nothing could have been further from his mind.

Top:
A Battle Scene: Tel-el-Kebir, 1883

Bottom:
Ted's first home-made Christmas card, 1879
He drew his own Christmas cards for the rest of his life

GREAT TIT

Top left:
Great Tit, undated

Top right:
Leptura Rubra,
found on
Lily of the Valley,
Birdlip, 1885

Bottom left:
Sallow Catkins,
The Crippetts, 1888

Bottom right:
Hazel Catkins,
The Crippetts, 1888

Left:
Gloucester from
Crickley Hill.
Painted in the period
1891-5

Bottom:
Cheltenham from
The Crippetts, 1895

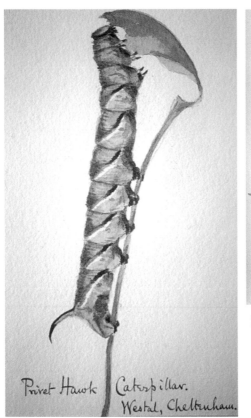

Privet Hawk Caterpillar.
Westal, Cheltenham.

White Dead Nettle.
Lamium Album.
Epping Forest. May 96
Fred Wilson.

Top left: Privet Hawk Moth caterpillar
Westal, July 1896
Top right: White Dead Nettle,
Epping Forest, May 1896
Bottom: Grass Snake,
surprised at being taken,
The Crippetts, March 1897

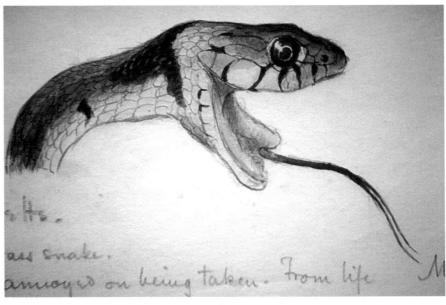

ass snake.
annoyed on being taken. From life

Top left: Leckhampton Church, c1898
Top right: Primrose from Cooper's Hill,
April 1898,
"That God should lay so much beauty
at our feet"
Bottom: Cock Chaffinch 1898

Left:
Showers coming down
the Rosdahl,
Norway, 1899

Bottom:
Ice Cutting on Davos Lake,
Switzerland, 1899

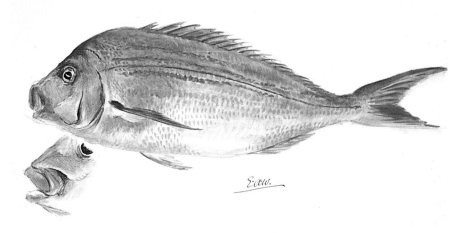

Fish caught on a line on the Agulhas Bank, South Africa. 35° 37½ S. 20° 34′ E. Oct: 15. 1901.

"Discovery" Antarctic Expedition.

E.A.W.

Top: Fish, caught off South Africa, 15 October 1901
Bottom left: Madeira
Bottom right: Trinidad Petrel

The Dormouse.
Plate for Bell's
British Mammals

Top:
Davos, c1900

Bottom left:
Ted, 1898

Bottom right:
L-R; Weatherhead, Woodlock and
Ted. Davos Platz, 1899

6. "Neck or Nothing"

*****
A short life with hard work is so much
preferable to a long one with comfort.
EAW
*****

In 1895, The International Geographical Congress had passed a resolution urging the scientific exploration of the Antarctic region, the Terra Australis Incognita, or Unknown Southern Land. It was not even certain if there was a continent present in the hole on the charts, although there was a great deal of informed speculation that there was. The challenge to explorers and scientists was to see if they could complete the map; could learn to understand the movements of the Southern Magnetic Pole; could reveal the secrets of Southern Hemisphere weather patterns; the list of important scientific and geographical questions, some of major economic consequence, was immense.

The first expeditions to sail in response to the Geographical Congress had been a Belgian Expedition, which was the first to winter in the pack ice of what is now the Amundsen Sea, aboard the ship *Belgica* (1897-99). The second was a private British expedition aboard the *Southern Cross* (1898-1900), which was the first expedition to winter on the Antarctic continent, at Cape Adare, on the northern most part of the western Ross Sea coast. Whilst these expeditions had provided much information on the conditions of the Antarctic winter, they had not answered many of the major scientific puzzles. The proposed British National Antarctic Expedition therefore became a part of a co-ordinated series of international expeditions aiming to do that: the British (*Discovery* 1901-04), Swedish (*Antarctic* 1901-04) and Germans (*Gauss* 1901-03), aimed to explore different coasts of Antarctica and ultimately exchanged much of their scientific data.

The British contribution to this quest for answers was brought about by the iron will of Sir Clements Markham, who had been pivotal in persuading the 1895 Geographical Congress to make its resolution. He now galvanised the Royal Geographical Society (of which he was President), the Royal Society, the Royal Navy and the British and Colonial Governments into action. He further forced the expedition plans through the humbug of committees and red tape into reality. The resulting British National Antarctic Expedition, aboard the *s.s.Discovery,* was to head for Victoria Land in the Ross Sea, first discovered by Sir James Clark Ross in 1841.

Black-bellied Storm Petrel

The suggestion, from Dr Sclater, that Ted should apply for this forthcoming expedition, was a considerable shock to him. On the one hand, the substantial changes in his life brought about by his experience with tuberculosis - in particular, his no longer desiring to become a member of the conventional medical establishment - meant that he was looking for a major change of direction into which he could channel his extraordinary creative energies. There seems little doubt that his childhood dream of becoming a 'naturalist' was still a powerful one that was slowly emerging into reality. On the other, however, was a large dose of pessimistic realism as to his choices. He was only just reaching the point of fully recovering from the tuberculosis and had given up all thought of going to work in Africa because of it: the thought of going to Antarctica instead must have seemed extraordinary to him. In addition, he had not yet completed his MB degree, he thought that his artwork was barely creditable and he was recently engaged. Ted seems to have had no hesitation in declining Dr Sclater's suggestion, or at least replying to it with serious reservations.

Dr Sclater appears to have understood Ted's self-effacing qualities rather well. A few days later he sent another letter stating that he was on the qualifying committee for the post of Junior Surgeon and Zoologist and it was his opinion that Ted was suitable. This strong encouragement, with the fact that Ted's thesis had been accepted during this exchange of letters, so that he was now in possession of his MB, helped to give him the necessary re-enforcement of self-confidence. He wrote to his father:

> It's an expensive thing this M.B., but I'm glad at last to have it in safe keeping, and if it lands me at the South Pole it will be well worth the expense. I am going for it for all I know because it is obviously a golden opportunity.

Once Ted had obtained Ory's approval, he accepted the invitation to apply and attended the various interviews with Professor Poulton and Mr [George] Murray in June 1900. These successful initial interviews led him to write to a friend that he was "practically certain" to be selected for the post. Later in the summer, Uncle Charlie decided to get involved in his nephew's welfare, sending a letter to his colleague Sir Clements Markham, to commend Ted's services to the enterprise. Further more, he showed Ted's artwork around the Royal Geographical Society.

Ted meanwhile, had remained in Cheltenham after a long summer holiday with Ory up at *The Crippetts*. He was now working at giving anaesthetics and performing minor surgery at the Cheltenham Hospital where he was a locum. In September, he was pleased to be appointed to the post of Junior House Surgeon. It must have been devastating for Ted when, at the end of September, his mother, much against her own wishes, decided to sell the lease of *The Crippetts*. The bailiff, Griffin, had lost the farm large sums of money through his "drunken carelessness" and his negligence meant that it had become unsustainable. On being sent to Andoversford to sell some pigs at this time, Griffin got so drunk that he fell out of the trap on his way home and hit his head. It ensured that he was not re-employed by the new owners and had to break rocks for a living instead. In the midst of this trauma, and within three weeks of his new hospital appointment, Ted cut himself in the course of his medical duties; he developed blood poisoning and an abscess of the axilla. Ted was forced to resign from his post and Ory sped to *Westal* to nurse him, where he lay in considerable pain.

So it was that on 22 November 1900, having been drained of pus and with his arm in a sling, at the wish of Sir Clements Markham, Professor Poulton and others, he went to London for an interview with the Antarctic Committee. It was decided to engage him, provided that his health recovered sufficiently. Captain Scott seems to have been particularly impressed with their first meeting and was keen that Ted should go with him, "practically appointing" him - but although Scott was appointed to command the expedition ship, *Discovery*, he was not yet in overall command of the expedition.

Shortly after Christmas, Ted's abscess required a second operation. Four days later, having been once more drained of pus, he was before the Medical Board of the Admiralty, who gave him three months to see if he would recover sufficiently. Professor Gregory who at this time was the head of the Scientific Staff on the expedition, accepted Ted's appointment anyway, provided that he would go at his own risk. Ted was ecstatic:

> I am going... they accept me in spite of everything if I will go at my own risks. I don't care in the least if I live or die - all is right and I am going; it will be the making of me.

At this point in time he was expecting to be landed from *Discovery* with Gregory and six others on the freezing edges of the known world, to be picked up again a year or two later. A few days after his appointment to the expedition, his excitement was further enhanced by news of his election as a Fellow of the Zoological Society of London.

Ted and Ory took lodgings at Pinner in Middlesex, from where he threw himself into the numerous preparations for the expedition: he designed the expedition crest; he started "working up" whales, dolphins and other weaknesses in his zoological repertoire; he brushed up his taxidermy; he prepared lists of required medical and scientific equipment; he practised the drawing and recognition of southern wildlife species, such as were known; and he started Antarctic work at the Natural History Museum by helping Hodgson (the appointed biologist to the expedition) to work on the messy

Expedition Crest

Antarctic specimens recently collected by the expedition aboard the *Southern Cross*. He wrote up the seals and painted the seal plates for the *Report on the Collections of Natural History made in the Antarctic regions during the Voyage of the Southern Cross* (1902) but was later to regret inaccuracies in the pictures because he had never seen one of these seals alive. Ory helped to speed his recovery whilst sewing and embroidering his sledging flag.

In April, Ted first met his future shipmates at the Royal Geographical Society, amongst them Ernest Shackleton whom he invited to lunch. Ted's first impression of him was not a good one "I don't care so much for him, he is so beastly scientific". Life became a whirl of dinners and luncheons, which he didn't much enjoy. He met several eminent polar explorers and started to read some of their books. Perhaps Ted's greatest concern, however, was the vexed question of whether or not to marry Ory before he left. His mother certainly thought that to marry at this time would be to take on unnecessary extra responsibilities. Ted, however, felt ready to risk anything:

> If the climate suits me, I shall come back more fit for work than ever, whereas if it doesn't, I think there is no fear of my coming back at all; I quite realise that it is kill or cure and have made up my mind, it shall be cure.

Ted and Ory set a tentative date for July, the eventual short notice meaning that many of their friends were unable to attend.

On 13 July Ted was finally rejected by the Admiralty Medical Board as unfit; he had recovered from the blood poisoning and so they had passed him as fit - until he informed them about his tuberculosis. Upon further examination they had decided that, although clear of the disease, the scar tissue that was still present rendered him unfit. Following Professor Gregory's resignation as Chief of the Scientific Staff, a major expedition of exploration was planned, rather than a small shore party, with Captain Scott himself now having working control of the expedition. Ted met Scott and discussed the matter of his medical condition with him. Scott, who had wanted him to come along ever since their first meeting, told him that the Medical Board's findings wouldn't make any difference as Ted had already undertaken to come at his own risk. A delighted Ted wired Ory at once to confirm that everything was going ahead.

Three days later, on 16 July 1901, Ted and Ory were married in the Church of St. Mary Magdalene at Hilton in Huntingdonshire (now in Cambridgeshire), where Ory's father, The Rev. F. A. Souper, was the incumbent. Ory was the picture of a bride, arriving in an open landau, drawn by two horses. The wedding received plenty of comment in the newspapers of Cheltenham and of Huntingdonshire.

> A fashionable wedding was solemnised at Hilton Parish Church, Hunts... the bride looked charming in a dress of white satin, trimmed with chiffon and lace, and she wore a tulle veil with a wreath of real orange blossoms. She also carried a bunch of white trumpet lilies...;

> ...peals were rung on the bells...the pathway over which the bride and bridegroom walked... was strewed with flowers by the schoolchildren...

Ted's brother Bernard, recently home from the war in South Africa, was the best man. Ted's sister, Polly, and Ory's sister, Constance, were bridesmaids. Ory's brother, Adrian, played the organ and Ted's friend the Rev. Leighton-Hopkins, performed the ceremony, assisted by Canon Escreet, Rector of Woolwich. Amongst many gifts was a silver epergne inscribed "Presented to E.A.Wilson on his marriage with Miss O. F. Souper, by Sir Clements Markham K.C.B. and the Commander, Officers and Scientific Staff of the *s.s.Discovery,* 16th July 1901." This gift was deeply touching to them both. Their "special day" was a very jolly party; Ted and Ory were beside themselves with happiness.

s.s Discovery

The following day, many of the wedding party visited *Discovery,* in the East India Docks, London, looking at Ted's future home and meeting the other members of the expedition. Ted was given special leave in the last days of preparation to be with Ory rather than the ship, a honeymoon of sorts, although he was still extremely busy. After an inspection at Cowes, by their Majesties King Edward VII and Queen Alexandra on 5 August, *Discovery* sailed from the Solent on 6 August 1901. Ory and other relatives sailed as far as Yarmouth where they were taken ashore by launch, Ory waving her hankie for all she was worth until *Discovery* was a mere speck on the horizon. Many family members did not think that they would ever see Ted again.

Discovery sailed via Madeira, South Trinidad, South Africa and Macquarie Island to New Zealand. It was a busy ship, conducting scientific programmes for much of the voyage. Ted was in his element. Ever demanding high standards from himself, he was far from happy with the products of his work, mostly because the conditions in which he was working precluded perfection. The rolling of the ship ensured that the preparation of specimens of bird or fish or plankton required considerable patience:

> Painting a bird which is swinging through 30 degrees every few seconds is trying, things won't stay as you put them. Your water is hung on a hook, your paper is pinned to a board, and you hold your paint box; you yourself are wedged into the bunk cupboard and kept there by a boot on the chest of drawers opposite. You put your paint-box down to settle a wing for the thirtieth time, and down it rattles and the paints go all over the cabin. You jump to save the paint box and the corner of the board tilts the water tin off the hook and it empties into a drawer full of clean drawing paper; while a running drip takes the opportunity of coming from the skylight on to your painting... It's a strange life teeming with quiet fun and everyone thoroughly enjoys it all...

Ted trained some of his fellow officers and crew to help with skinning and preserving specimens. Petty Officer Cross, in particular, became quite expert. Often the work was a race against time and had to be done quickly to save the specimens from the heat of the tropics or the deluges of salt water rushing the decks in rougher weather. Even with assistance, he was unable to rescue everything. The day after leaving South Trinidad was particularly busy:

> Up at 6a.m. painting the heads and feet of all my birds. Same all the morning, and then! my word, skinned hard on till nearly 10.30 pm with intervals for eating... We had to hurry on all we could, because they had already begun to stink by the evening. I put four young terns into formalin, as we had no time to skin them. The fish were all far too gone by the morning even to paint. They were blown out and the colours all altered or gone.

Dry Sketching Box

Despite his modest doubts, however, the work, which Ted sent home whenever possible, was to receive quiet acclaim in scientific circles, so much so, that a new species of petrel found on South Trinidad was named after him, although many years later it was subsumed as a sub-species of the Trinidad or Herald Petrel. The extraordinary amount of work which he was achieving was also being noticed by his colleagues. Captain Scott particularly admired Ted's productivity, adaptability, inventiveness and willingness to help all aboard in often unobtrusive ways. These inventions of Ted's often ended up having dual purposes for work and pleasure:

> The sea this afternoon was simply splendid, an immense swell and breaking everywhere. I spent most of the day on deck. Have made a bad weather sketching box which I hang round my neck and can sketch comfortably in it even when it rains and blows a gale and spray comes all over one; the paper keeps comparatively dry - so; The Skipper thinks it's an excellent plan, and we use it for a barrel organ in our impromptu theatricals on the bridge...

Captain Scott

The amount of fun which was had on board, in between all the hard work, is often overlooked in the histories of such expeditions. Shackleton and Ted soon became firm friends through their mutual delight in larking about, Shackleton having a poem, ditty or amusing anecdote for every occasion. Lieutenant Charles Royds, the most accomplished piano player on board, was also to become a firm friend of Ted's, his eloquent playing a balm for Ted's soul. Yet Ted felt that Captain Scott understood him perhaps the best of all, although they could not, as yet, be described as having a deep friendship. Ted admired the fact that Scott mucked in with everything rather than standing on his rank, was very interested in all of the scientific work taking place on board, was innovative, supremely fair and deeply honest. The one aspect that he didn't like, although learned to tolerate, was Scott's impatience - the product of a naval education that expected much and expected it done yesterday. Amidst all the jollity, the officers acquired nicknames, Ted becoming known as 'Bill' or 'Billy', much to the annoyance of some of his old friends back home, who thought 'Ginger' to be superior.

Despite the hard work and the constant jesting, however, Ted, at least initially, felt a deep lack in not being able to talk to anybody aboard about the deeper things of life. His old friends and his soul mate were far away. Naval life was something of a shock to him, particularly the more rugged language and attitudes of the lower deck and the uncontemplated assumptions of some of the junior officers. After his years at Cambridge and working in the slums, however, he took it in his stride, although his occasional wry comments meant that he was known by some as 'Bill the cynic'. In his usual quiet way, he would slip off and read to himself the daily services and pray - away from the teasing comments of his fellows.

Between Cape Town and Macquarie Island *Discovery* sailed south to the edge of the pack ice, a brief experience of the cold new world that was to be home for two years. Ted was staggered by its scale and beauty:

> ...now we had loose ice all round us and here and there great frozen hummocks, where slabs the size of kitchen tables were thrown one on the other anyhow and so frozen, with every hollow and crack and crevice a perfect miracle of blue and green light and then came the ice birds... Well, I couldn't leave the upper deck - the whole outlook was so fascinating and from early morning till 11pm when it was still quite light, many of us remained spell-bound barring meals!

From the ice they turned north to Macquarie Island, where Ted offered the Pilot a bottle of liqueur if he could persuade the Captain to stop for collecting. It didn't take much persuasion. Here, Ted was to make his first real acquaintance with penguins, on which he was to become an authority.

On arrival at Lyttelton, New Zealand, Ted did a lot of work in the Canterbury Museum in Christchurch before shipping the collections home. He wrote long letters. In particular, he warned his family and friends to ignore the newspaper reports about the expedition, which he thought distinctly inaccurate - no concern being given to the truth, nor to people's feelings, in the desperate rush to sell newspapers; he was disgusted. His diary too, written for the family in England, he posted back to Ory. During his time in Christchurch and Lyttelton, he made a large number of scientific contacts and new friends. He thought that the social whirl of parties and dinners, which constantly interrupted his scientific work, was overwhelmingly generous but he found them wearing. Ted was not unhappy when it was time to sail south.

As *Discovery* left Lyttelton, huge crowds cheered them off. Just after the last steamers of hoorahing sightseers had wished them well and turned back, the expedition suffered its first casualty. One of the sailors, Bonner, fell from the rigging.

Discovery quietly slipped into Dunedin to take on more coal, here they also buried their comrade. They sailed from Port Chalmers on 24 December 1901 bound for the unexplored lands of the Great White South. Any anxiety that Ted might have had about his health failing again, stopping him from going all the way, had proved groundless and melted away. He was fitter than ever and putting on weight. Life at sea agreed with him. In any case, now there would be no turning back. The New Zealand coast faded from view:

Crow's Nest

Now, neck or nothing, we are fairly started, thank God, and by His grace we shall do something worth the doing before we sight New Zealand and civilisation again.

As his son was sailing south, Ted's father gave a paper before the Cheltenham Natural Science Society, outlining the plans, the questions and the conjectures of the current phase of Antarctic exploration. ETW was extremely proud, if anxious, that Ted was amongst the explorers. They wouldn't know for many months, what, if any progress was being made. The long silence began.

Top left:
Amusing scenes in the garden at Westal -
Ted tries on his officers furs for the forthcoming
expedition
Top right:
"Urgent Dispatches" Ted and Ory writing letters
in the garden at Westal
Bottom:
16 July 1901, On their Wedding Day: L-R Polly;
Ted; Ory; Constance

Top left: Larking about, Ted and a Discovery life-ring
Top right: Ted's cabin aboard Discovery
Bottom: Landing on South Trinidad (Ted is at centre-right).

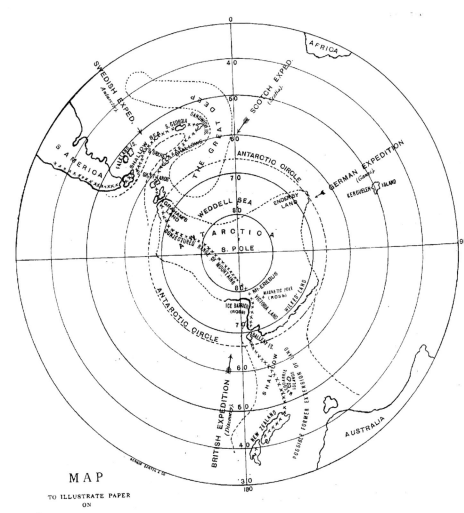

MAP

ANTARCTICA

BY

E. T. WILSON.

Map of Antarctica
showing the proposed routes of the European expeditions
including Discovery,
From Edward Thomas Wilson's paper

7. "Farthest South".

It is almost impossible to imagine what it must have been truly like to sail towards the unknown and the sort of courage that it must have taken. Even if we were to launch astronauts today for Mars, they would know more about where they were heading and have better communications with the World than the officers and men who sailed aboard *Discovery.*

> ...a whole year must pass now before a word of news can come of all that is most dear in life, and we must feed our happiness with hopes and recollections and trust God. Well, I know well, that three weeks with my Ory is food enough for three years' hope, and three years' happiness. God keep her.

They sailed through the windswept Southern Ocean, where the albatross soars for mile upon endless mile, through the chilled whispers of the ice pack and into the Ross Sea. Heading south, they were soon at the edge of geographical ignorance, its sentinel one of the world's most breathtaking wonders, the Great Ice Barrier:

> Then came the cliff of the Ice Barrier stretching away like a coast line, irregularly with one or two large bays and promontories, for near 60 miles as far as one could see with glasses. Then came the ice plain on which was setting a glorious sun and miles and miles and miles of smooth ice...

This extraordinary wall of ice had been discovered by Ross - and would eventually be re-named after him as the Ross Ice Shelf - but its full extent was still unclear. They sailed along the fringe of it collecting specimens, still in awe of the vast icescape which they were seeing, the ice edge averaging 100 feet (30 metres) in height where it met the ocean. They discovered the eastern termination of the Barrier, naming the new found land for King Edward VII and, unable to go further, turned the ship back to the west. Along the return route a balloon ascent was made to survey the distant view, the first flight made by human beings in the Antarctic, but no land could be seen. They returned to the

*Wandering
Albatross*

vicinity of the volcanoes Mounts Erebus and Terror, where a sheltered site in which to spend the winter was sought and found at the end of McMurdo Bay, soon to be re-named McMurdo Sound when fresh discoveries proved them to be on an island (Ross Island).

Ted was frantically busy during the whole of this time. He was constantly on deck, collecting specimens of albatrosses, penguins or other seabirds, of seals and whatever other life they encountered. These needed painting, skinning and dissecting. He was further called to the deck to sketch every new piece of land that was seen and soon had pencil sketches of almost the entire coast of Victoria Land, panoramas that even today are extraordinary for their detail, accuracy and length - amounting to over 100 feet (30 metres) of sketches. Using his colour memorisation notation he was able to defer the painting of many of the watercolours until the months of comparative inactivity during the winter.

The ship was to serve as Winter Quarters. Huts were built ashore for scientific instruments and emergency accommodation. Once these were established, the first tentative exploratory sledge journeys were undertaken. Ted was sent with Shackleton and Ferrar (the geologist) to make the first such journey: to discover what lay south of White Island. Almost every new rock or frosted horizon was a new discovery, never before beheld by human eyes. They learned, on the job, the realities of cold weather exploration that they had read about in books or discussed with old hands. They suffered from mild cases of frostbite. Ted, having read that the treatment for frostbite was to rub it with snow, rubbed the skin off Shackleton's ears. It was a sharp lesson but they kept their senses of humour, attained the summit of the island and returned safely to the ship. The return of another of the exploratory journeys at this time was not so lucky. The party was caught by a blizzard in which one seaman, Vince, fell over the edge of a cliff to his death. The youngest member of the crew, who was lost at this time, re-appeared at the ship 44 hours later, apparently none the worse for his adventure. Ted was kept busy in the medical department treating everything from frostbite to a broken leg.

On 31 March, Ted set out on a further journey with Scott, Armitage (Navigator and Second in Command), Ferrar, and a large party of the crew. He noted that it was the same day that the hounds were to meet at the Queen's Hotel and draw Crippetts Wood. He often thought of home; because his diary was written for the family he often wrote of the Gloucestershire countryside around *The Crippetts*. It was his way of giving metaphorical access to the strange land and so to some extent to allow the family to share in his adventures. The aim of this sledging trip was to establish a depot for the next season's exploration work. The only drawing that the dogs were to do was of sledges. It was bitterly cold, as low as -47°F (-44°C); it was too late in the season for sledging. After three days they deposited the provisions and returned to Winter Quarters. The long Antarctic winter was upon them.

In the seemingly endless darkness and howling blizzards of an Antarctic winter, with a small, disparate group of officers and men more or less confined in conditions of bare comfort, miles from home, it is unsurprising that there was a certain amount of tension on board, particularly when there were old rivalries between the Royal and Merchant Navies to be endured. Ted was glad that they were all kept very busy with scientific work, daily chores, compulsory exercise and entertainments in the form of debates, lectures and theatrical performances at the 'Royal Terror Theatre'.

> If one couldn't work and hadn't more than one can get through, this life would be unbearable. Men don't improve when they live together alone, cut off from all the better half of humanity that encourages decency and kindliness. Some of our mess have quite dropped the mask and are not so attractive in their true colouring.

Ted found living in close proximity to naval men to be trying, his temper stretched, but he refused to give in to it. Instead he regarded it as a testing ground, a "hard school". It was a further step on his path of ascetic self-control. He said that he wouldn't have missed the experience for the world. Perhaps the person whom Ted found it most difficult to get along with, however, and he was far from alone in this, was Koettlitz, the senior surgeon. Ted found it difficult to like his brand of scientific determinism and apparent lack of work. Ted, however, deliberately set out to keep the peace and to smooth over all such frictions.

> ... a little bit of peace-making is wanted here and there in this community of men, some of whom are not inclined to live peaceably with one another. We have had very few rows, but friction is continual between some parties ...

Many of Ted's companions thought that he was one of the beneficial influences on the ship, particularly in the Ward Room, helping to keep the friction confined to people's thoughts in diaries and letters, so that it only occasionally broke out into the open. Additionally, the expedition, being largely naval, was run by Scott as such. Bernacchi, the physicist, who had previously wintered with the *Southern Cross* expedition, thought that the smoother relationships throughout the winter on *Discovery* were very much to do with the formality of the naval routines encouraging enforced politeness, however artificial. *Discovery* came through the winter far more successfully than either of the two preceding expeditions to winter in the Antarctic, and better than many that were to follow.

As well as frictions there were of course many friendships. Ted spent hours talking with Charles Royds or singing duets with him at the piano. He also enjoyed frequent walks and talks with Shackleton. They often went up the 900 feet (275 metres) to the top of Crater Hill to read the thermometer at the outlying weather station, the old volcanic cone at the top of the hill being "about as big as Montpellier Gardens". In Cheltenham, however, the average air temperature was +48°F (+9°C), a far cry from the temperatures on the top of Crater Hill, between -

20°F and -40°F (-29°C and -40°C), in which Ted would stand and make sketches of the moonlit winter landscape. It was under such frigid conditions that he stood and sketched the first accurate images of the Aurora Australis, or Southern Lights. This was not a process without a great deal of pain, as sketching required removing his hands from his gloves, warming them up again after a few minutes when the cold had removed all sensation, and then sketching again. Frost-nip was a regular risk. Ted also spent a great deal of time with Shackleton producing the *South Polar Times,* the shipboard magazine which Shackleton edited and Ted mostly illustrated. He also regularly spent time with some of the seamen,

Silhouette Shackleton

particularly Petty Officer Cross, who helped him to skin and prepare penguins and other scientific specimens. There were also regular walks to kill seals for food. In addition to this work, Ted regularly tasted all of the tinned milk and food to ensure that it wasn't tainted (tainted food was thought to be the cause of scurvy), looked after the ventilation of the living spaces, worked up his paintings and zoological notes and, according to Scott, "performed a hundred and one kindly offices for all on board". More and more, people came to Ted when they needed to laugh, chat or wanted advice. For Ted, it was all a part of the working out of God's will in the far flung corners of His Creation.

For Ted, the biggest surprise of the winter was when Scott called him into his cabin and asked him to accompany him on the attempt to reach the Farthest South the following sledging season. They discussed whether to be a party of two or three; Ted wanted three. Scott chose Shackleton as the third man, apparently to please what he thought would be Ted's wishes, knowing that they were close friends. Ted knew that to go on this journey was Shackleton's greatest desire. In fact, he was unsure whether Shackleton was physically up to it. For the sake of his friend, he said nothing: "He is so keen to go... that he will carry it through".

The advance supporting parties left the ship on 30 October 1902 followed on 2 November by Scott, Shackleton and Wilson, driving the dog teams. They headed south over the Great Ice Barrier, determined to get as far towards the Pole as they could. Scott hoped to reach as far as 85° South. Four days out Shackleton started a persistent cough. On the 15th the last supporting party was sent back to the ship. The dogs had been pulling well and they could travel faster without waiting for the supporting parties. Everything was looking very promising. Almost immediately, however, things started to go wrong. Now with an extra (sixth) sledge in train, the dogs wouldn't pull and so they started to relay their supplies, covering fifteen miles (27kms) for every 5 miles (9kms) which they made to the south. Every day, the dogs got weaker and weaker. They started to pull the sledges with the dogs, trying everything they knew to help them and yet being constantly frustrated. On 21 November they sighted new land and altered course slightly to map and sketch it. They would be able to start defining the inland limits of the Great Ice Barrier. Everything, however, depended on the dogs. Mixed with this worry was the sheer

Sledge Dog

excitement of what they were seeing. New lands and breathtaking new sights, parhelia, perihelia, mock suns and showers of ice crystals on a scale they had never seen before. They pressed on. The dogs started to pass blood and show signs of dysentery. They started to die. Concluding that the diet of the dogs, dried fish from Norway that had been recommended by Nansen, was at fault, they started to feed the dead to the remaining strong dogs, and then to kill the weak to feed to the strong. It was of immediate benefit. The job of butcher eventually fell to Ted alone. The men too started to get very hungry:

> We are really doing very heavy work on very low rations but are all very fit. I think a lot on the march of the hot summer days at the Crippetts when one could go down into the cool dairy and find unlimited fresh creamy thick milk and a large common "destroyer" cake. Fresh milk - how I long for a big jug of it!

They had pleasant dreams about food that became nightmares upon waking. Realising that they could not make it as far south as they had hoped, in mid-December they deposited a large portion of their supplies which ended the necessity of relaying. They pushed further south. They were close enough in to the land now for Ted to regularly sketch the newly discovered coast line. Scott took angular measurements of the coast and of Ted's drawings and found them to be astonishingly accurate. Ted removed his snow goggles to make such sketches and suffered an immense amount of pain from snow blindness (effectively sunburn of the eye), sometimes having to sledge blindfolded. During these periods he had vivid day-dreams:

> ...suggested by the intense heat of the sun I think. Sometimes I was in beech woods, sometimes in fir woods, sometimes in the Birdlip woods... And the swish-swish of the ski was as though one's feet were brushing through dead leaves, or cranberry undergrowth or heather or juicy bluebells... it was delightful.

They sighted new mountain ranges even further to the south and pushed on. It wasn't always warm: the slightest breeze or the sun dipping to the horizon meant cold conditions. They reached their "Farthest South" on 30 December a latitude of 82° 17' South (estimated from Scott's sights at their lunch camp), far short of the 85° South Scott had hoped to achieve. Ted thought that this was more than made up for by the discovery of new land, with mountains from 10,000 to 13,000 feet (3,000 to 4,000 metres) in height, instead of a vast icy plain. They flew their flags. Scott named the furthest visible inlet for Shackleton, the Cape for Ted. The coast was charted to 83° South. Ted and Scott went for a quick ski run to the south of their camp to see if they could see anything more but because of thick weather, they could not. The following day they tried to reach solid land to obtain geological specimens but were foiled by high pressure ridges and crevasses.

On 1 January they returned north. They soon had no dogs remaining and man-hauled the sledges, sometimes assisted by the use of a sail made from the floor cloth of their tent. The voyage back was to be a race against time. Scurvy had first made its appearance on the *Discovery* expedition during the spring sledging season. By stopping the use of some tinned meat and replacing it with more fresh meat the outbreaks were eliminated. When Scott, Shackleton and Ted started to show definite signs of having the disease at their furthest point south, they took similar precautions, stopping the bacon ration on the assumption that this was tainted and using their 'fresh' seal meat supplies instead. Unfortunately, the seal meat had been both dried and cooked, so had little or no vitamin C content (they could not have known this as vitamins were still undiscovered). Their 'fresh' food therefore did little to combat the scurvy and the condition continued to deteriorate. By the end, Ted wrote that he had enough notes and experience of the disease in every stage to write an MD, if he ever wanted one. Shackleton, in particular, suffered badly, scurvy apparently exacerbating his already existing cough. he started to cough blood and came close to collapse. It looked as if he wouldn't pull through. He couldn't help to pull the sledge. Ted's knee started to cause him pain; he gritted his teeth, there was no choice. It was a close run thing. On 3 February they arrived back at the ship, having been spotted from far off and greeted by an increasing number of officers and men. When they reached the ship they found it:

3 Men on Skis

> ... decorated from top to toe with flags and all the ship's company up the rigging round the gangway ready to cheer us, which they did most lustily as we came on board.

The first great penetration into the heart of Antarctica was completed. They removed clothes that had been on since November, had a bath and a huge meal. All Ted wanted to do was lie on his bunk and chat to Charles Royds.

The Southern Journey cemented Ted's friendship with both his companions. Shackleton and Ted had been good friends for some time and, at least for the first part of the journey, they were as thick as thieves, subtly combining to counter Scott's impatience. Ted was able to write that they had Scott "well in hand".

Ted remained close to Shackleton throughout, nursing him when he was unwell on the return journey and, with Scott, saved his life. Emily Shackleton later wrote:

> We owe so much to your son for all the care he took of Ernest when he was so ill - and Ernest always spoke of him with such adoration and affection.

The relationship that changed most dramatically on the Southern Journey was Ted's relationship with Scott. On the return journey, Ted, in his words, "had it out" with Scott. Whether this was sparked by a particular incident with Scott or not, we will probably never know. The two of them talked alone for hours, over several days. What was discussed is unknown but it seems unlikely that much was left out because their relationship was forged from one of mutual respect to a deep and lasting friendship based on a profound understanding, each of the other. It is said that, after this journey, Scott's eyes would light up at the mention of Ted's name. Scott's sister later wrote, "My brother loved him, there was a tender sympathy between them always". That mutual love was forged on this journey.

Shackleton's illness was more serious than simple scurvy and it seems unlikely that Scott had any choice but to send him home on the relief ship, *Morning*, which had arrived with mail and fresh supplies. Their relationship upon return to the ship, as written up in other people's diaries, does not have the appearance of mutual simmering resentment, as some have suggested: Scott was jumping up and down cooking Shackleton sardines on toast. Ted noted that Shackleton's serious coughing was brought on by the approach of southern blizzards, as was his own rheumatism which was as good as a barometer. Under those circumstances, to have kept Shackleton south would have been an unconscionable risk.

The ice having failed to break out from around *Discovery* left her frozen in for another Antarctic winter; *Morning* returned to New Zealand alone. The second winter passed much as the first, although more peacefully. Bernacchi took over the editing of the *South Polar Times*. By the end of the winter Ted had produced over 200 watercolours and sketched detailed panoramas of the newly discovered coast from the Southern Journey. In Shackleton's absence, he walked to the top of Crater Hill alone, refusing company. He was anxious for the spring, when he would be able to continue his "proper sphere of work" and finally have the chance to go and study the most important biological discovery of the expedition so far: Lieutenant Skelton, on one of the 1902 spring sledging parties under Lieutenant Royds, had found an Emperor Penguin nesting colony at Cape Crozier on the eastern end of Ross Island, the first one discovered.

On 7 September 1903 Ted finally got his wish, to leave the ship for Cape Crozier. Royds led the party since he already knew the way. To Ted's surprise they found that the chicks were already well grown. They secured several deserted eggs and Petty Officer Cross brought two live chicks away with them which he and Ted fed on chewed seal meat. Low temperatures from -49°F to -61°F (-45°C to -52°C) caused them to return to the ship rapidly. The chicks kept Ted up for many nights, clamouring for him to chew them some food and feed them; though he and Cross were doting parents the chicks eventually died. Ted made a second journey to Cape Crozier in October with P.O. Cross and Leading Stoker Whitfield. Ted was as esteemed by many of the seamen as he was by many of the officers, perhaps in part because he treated them with the same care as he treated all, sharing with them his 'officers treats' when they sledged together. On this journey, Ted was the first to witness the post-breeding migration of the Emperor Penguins out to sea on ice-floes. These first scientific notes of the breeding cycle of the Emperor Penguin, made from observations from earlier sledging parties and from his own notes, led Ted to a conclusion that seemed so unbelievable that he could scarcely credit it. The Emperor Penguin had to lay and incubate its eggs during the Antarctic Winter. It was an extraordinary discovery.

Penguin Chick

Ted went on several other relatively local sledge journeys during the summer. Scott had gone on another great exploratory journey to the west. Shortly after his return the two friends went camping to Cape Royds for some peace and quiet amongst a newly discovered Adelie Penguin rookery, the most southerly in the world. From here, whilst discussing the possibilities for another season, they were the first to see two relief ships arrive, *Morning* and *Terra Nova*. They brought the shocking orders to abandon *Discovery* if the ice did not free her. Fortunately, the swell of the ocean eventually broke the ice and they were soon on their way to New Zealand. They called in at the Auckland Islands on their way north, the first green trees that they had seen in two years.

They received a rapturous welcome into Lyttelton... and there Ted was reunited with his beloved Ory. She had run over the hills to the Port of Lyttelton on news of the ship and went out to greet him aboard a tug. Ory had spent a year in New Zealand, getting to know "the cream" of New Zealand Society, as Ted thought. He joked that she would make a Society man of him yet - but he found the whirl of social events to welcome them back to civilisation overwhelming. After much of his work was taken care of, Ted and Ory had their long delayed honeymoon, a three week trip through the North Island of New Zealand. It captivated them and they were sorry to leave. Ory sailed home aboard *Tongariro* and Ted on *Discovery*, which sailed via South America, the Falkland Islands and the Azores, returning to England on 10 September 1904. With Ted's parents, Ory was there to meet him. A relieved ETW was delighted that:

> ...he was once more amongst us looking the picture of health and much bronzed... it is indeed a treat to hear him tell of all the terrible sufferings and perils which he had undergone.

Once ashore, they faced another round of social receptions. The one which Ted minded the least was on 26 September at Westal, where he was welcomed back to Cheltenham with a large 'at home'. Many dozens of friends came to see him and to view his Antarctic sketches. "It was a very joyful occasion and one's heart was full of thankfulness," wrote his father. Ory was radiantly happy. Ted was home.

Falkland Island Steamer Duck

Top:
Farthest South, Ted stands opposite the Cape named for him
Cape Wilson 82 degrees 17 min S

Emperor Penguin

Top:
The Southern Party Returns
(with Ted's notes)

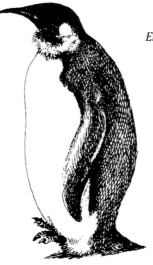

Emperor Penguin

Shackleton.   Capt. Scott.   Wilson.
On arrival at the ship after 3 months Southern Sledge Journey.
Nov. 2. 02 — Feb. 2. 03.   82°17′S.

Top: L-R Shackleton,Scott and Ted on return from the Farthest South (with Ted's notes)
Bottom left: Ted suffering from Scurvy, on return from Farthest South
Bottom right: Ted on Return to Westal

Top: Discovery in Winter Quarters
Bottom: Emperor Penguin, Farthest East, 31 January 1902

*Cape Wadworth,
Coulman Island*

Top:
Hut Point 11 April 1911

Bottom:
An Iceberg off Cape Evans, 1-11 September 1911

The Barn Owl.
Plate for a proposed edition
of Yarrell's British Birds

8. "A Grouse by every Post"

*****

Principles are the laws of life
which each person makes for himself,
and the best people are those whose
principles are so strong that they resist
every temptation to anything lower,
yet so pliant that they readily give
way to anything higher.
Like a cog-wheel with a catch,
they can always be screwed a turn higher
and never drop to where they were before.
EAW

*****

Black Grouse

Ted was extremely busy from the moment his feet touched English soil. In addition to the social whirl, in which he engaged himself as little as possible, he was busy working on the expedition collections in the Natural History Museum, amongst them the first exciting scientific specimens of Emperor Penguin eggs and chicks. He was also soon organising, with Skelton (who had been the main photographer on the expedition), an exhibition of pictures at the Bruton Gallery in London. To keep both the Royal Geographical Society (whom he regarded as temporary 'owners' of the paintings) and the gallery owners happy, Ted agreed to reproduce his expedition watercolours for purchase. This was an undertaking that he was to regret deeply. The exhibition opened on 7 November 1904, to coincide with Captain Scott's expedition lecture at the Royal Albert Hall, and was a huge success, crowds of people having to be turned away from the door. Even the aged Sir Joseph Hooker, who had sailed to the Antarctic with Ross, as his Assistant Surgeon, went to see it and was impressed by Ted's paintings. The exhibition's display of the first images of Emperor Penguin chicks was particularly popular, starting a long fascination amongst the British public. Ted started to become famous; he wasn't impressed. Over eighty reproductions were ordered, which he duly painted over the next six months, considering some of the 'copies' to be better than the 'originals'. The exhibition arrived in Cheltenham in February 1905, where large crowds once again lined up to see it.

In order to undertake most of this work, which was London based, Ted and Ory took rooms, and later a house, at Bushey, Hertfordshire. He rarely had time to investigate the marshy hollows and woods that surrounded him, although he loved to do nothing better. He also saw his family less than he would have liked, although they were very much at the centre of post-expedition activity. With its connections to Ted, Cheltenham developed an appetite for things Antarctic, with *Westal* a focal point. Captain Scott, who was engaged on a national speaking tour, stayed at *Westal* in early December 1904, lecturing in Cheltenham twice on 10 December and in Cirencester the following day, his motor car getting caught in a snow storm, so that he didn't return to *Westal* until late. Ted's parents nevertheless had several interesting talks with him before he left for Dublin. Edward Thomas found him to be "clever, unassuming and amusing". As Ted started the major task of writing up his share of the scientific reports of the expedition, he sent his scientific papers to his father for comment before submitting them for publication, an act which showed the tremendous esteem in which he held him and which also meant that the local Natural Science Society was kept abreast of developments. Work connected with the publication of the expedition reports, *South Polar Times,* picture albums and the like, would occupy much of Ted's time for the next four years. It also kept him in regular touch with Scott and forged one of Ted and Ory's greatest friendships - with the publisher Reginald Smith (of Smith, Elder and Co.) and his wife.

In addition to these major projects Ted also started working on the illustrations for books on the expedition by Scott and by Armitage, he made lantern slides for Royds, and painted a picture for the King which was presented to His Majesty on 18 December, when he and his ship-mates went to Buckingham Palace to receive the Polar Medal from the King. Ted also started to give immensely popular lectures, many at prestigious scientific and learned societies and also at public schools, including his old school at Cheltenham College (in November 1905). Laced with his dry humour and his impressions of penguins, his direct conversational style won him many ovations and accolades. For Ted lecturing took particular courage, however; he preferred to cross crevasses than face a room full of people. His intense nervousness overcame him on one occasion at St. George's Hospital where on rising to reply to an after-dinner eulogy, he became so overwhelmed by the accolade of his medical colleagues, that he sat down again immediately, unable to utter a word. It got to the point where it wasn't unknown for him to carefully administer to himself a mild sedative before a talk.

Amongst Ted's most important addresses were those that he gave on the subject of penguin conservation. A growing industry was boiling penguins for their oil, particularly on Macquarie Island, a matter which Ted raised at the annual general meeting of the Royal Society for the Protection of Birds (RSPB) and in an address to the International Ornithological Congress in 1905. This started a process that resulted in the trade being banned - although not until many years after Ted's death and only through Apsley Cherry-Garrard continuing to pursue the matter. The world might well not enjoy penguins in the numbers which it now has if it hadn't been for Ted having strong views on the subject and making them known. His deep love for nature, and particularly for birds, was involving him more and more in the growing conservation movement. He had seen what was happening in New Zealand with regard to the rate at which species were vanishing and was greatly concerned. He had applied to everyone he could think of in New Zealand to become a government scientist there, or a warden on one of their two island wildlife sanctuaries. He was very keen to go and do what he could to help and to record the vanishing birds with his paints - but no post was forthcoming, much to his disappointment. As a result of his observations Ted had come around to the point of condemning wildlife collecting entirely, except for strictly scientific purposes which he regarded as an unfortunate necessity. Likewise, he had come to regard many blood sports, as opposed to ordinary hunting, as an activity that should be outlawed in a civilised society. These views were very 'modern' views for Edwardian England and still very much a minority opinion.

It is perhaps ironic, then, that the next big project would involve him, in a peripheral way, with blood sports. After an address to the British Ornithological Union in March 1905, he was introduced to Lord Lovat, who was Chairman of the Board of Agriculture's Commission on the Investigation of Grouse Disease. An unknown disease was ravaging the grouse stocks on Britain's moors, and the Inquiry was to find out what it was and to stop it. Two field observers had attempted the task but neither had solved the problem. They were looking for a new 'Field Observer' for six months of the year who was also a bacteriologist and doctor. Since this left him free for the other six months of the year to paint and pursue other work, Ted willingly accepted the position. The project was to involve far more work on his part than he had ever anticipated.

Whiskered Bat

At around the same time, Ted was approached by an old Cambridge friend, Major Barrett Hamilton, to illustrate his new edition of Bell's *A History of British Mammals* (1910) - the standard work on the subject. Ted was then approached by Mr Eagle Clarke who asked him to illustrate his new edition of the standard work, Yarrell's *A History of British Birds.* This was a project very close to Ted's heart and greatly excited him. Ted agreed to execute both illustrative projects in the six month intervals between his grouse work. It was whilst painting bats for the mammal illustrations that Ted recognised a rather rare flea. On attending to her husband's call for help, Ory was left to hold the pencil under strict instructions not to let the flea hop away, whilst Ted found a tube of spirit for the specimen. The incident, later portrayed in the film, *Scott of the Antarctic,* is a good example of the extraordinary breadth of Ted's scientific knowledge.

In August 1905, he was persuaded to join the rest of the family for a holiday in the south west of Ireland, where his parents had taken a house for a month. He took a great deal of work with him and did some of the book illustrations whilst there, particularly of species already rare on mainland Britain. With resonances of *Crippetts* days, it was to be the last of the great Wilson family holidays, where long days were spent sketching, bird-nesting, botanising and picnicking; Ted's parents were ageing - ETW was now over 70; Ted would never again escape his work. The rugged scenery was a refreshing change and the entire family rejoiced in having some length of time together in the bracing country air.

Every dead grouse found on British moors was sent to Ted for dissection and examination. By 1906 they were accepting delivery of "a grouse by every post". In the end he dissected over 2,000 birds and muttered that he even skinned them in his sleep. Ted tried to make a museum skin of every specimen, which also had to be weighed, measured and to have its crop contents and intestines analysed. Most of his work was done at home or in cold hotel rooms up and down the country. On one occasion, in his rush to catch the train, he left "a bag full of slugs" behind in his room. Quite what the chambermaid thought of her slimy discovery he dreaded to think. His notes were often written up on the train. Occasionally he borrowed a laboratory to work in. Even *Westal* became filled with grouse feathers during his visits. As the birds took over their lives Ory became Ted's voluntary assistant taking notes or reading to him whilst he sketched and skinned. On occasions, Ted went to visit the grouse moors, striding across the open country, outpacing even the gamekeepers and gillies. With them he would hold long conversations about the virtues of not slaughtering 'vermin' and especially birds of prey, (a problem the RSPB is trying to resolve to this day); if this was met, as it often was, with a hard entrenchment, they soon discovered that Ted knew as much about the habits of game or its predators as they did. He became as respected by the gamekeepers as he was by the landowners, who started to go out of their way to assist him. On one such occasion, Ted was astonished to receive a reply to a report on the dissection of two grouse informing him that those birds had been intended for consumption and not for dissection. It wasn't long before he had identified the cause of grouse disease, a small threadworm *(Trichostrongylus tenuis)* which crawls up the heather, infesting the dew drops which the grouse ingests whilst eating and drinking, which then kills the birds by interrupting their digestive processes. The search for the origin of the nematode (thus the bag of slugs) was to take considerably longer but was eventually solved.

Perhaps in anticipation of a quick resolution to this work, Ted was already looking around for other projects. Despite his successes and wide acclaim for his achievements, Ted was disturbed by the notion that his was merely a hand to mouth existence. This worry struck to the heart of deep contradictions in his life at this time - highlighting the struggle for him between personal freedom, responsibility and the demands of social convention. The rigidity and expectations of the class system in Britain at this time were very powerful. Ted was a part of this, he couldn't not be - everyone is determined to an extent by social norms. As a member of the

Pine Marten

upper middle classes - proudly and consciously so - he had a certain amount of freedom but also a high number of expectations and demands placed upon him, most of which he brushed aside in his dislike of 'Society'. However, his days of solitary ascetic rigidity were over, Ted was settling into married life with Ory. Together they lived a simple if not Spartan life: they preferred not to have servants, for example, sharing the household chores to a degree almost unheard of in this era. As a married man there were, however, heavy social expectations that were new to Ted and with which he now wrestled. It seems certain that he and Ory contemplated having a family. Social norms demanded that a married man support such a family with a steady and regular income. His upper-middle class identity further required that this be acquired through a 'career' or 'profession'; and he was aware too that as an 'amateur' he was open to the cynicism of critics. Responsibility and duty were concepts that Ted had always felt strongly about, tying in with his strict personal codes of honour and conduct, based on a deep understanding of the Christian way of life. So it was that Ted fretted about being an "amateur potterer", not really having a career in anything. He dreaded drifting into becoming a General Practitioner or a "Museum Illustrator" out of financial necessity and looked around for some other form of "regular billet". At odds with these pressures were his rich natural talents and love of freedom, his ascetic and deeply spiritual life, the fact that although he was a product of his time in terms of class and class consciousness, he constantly overturned the norms of his day in his endless struggle with Truth and didn't actually fit into the role that conventionality expected of him at all.

So it was that in August 1906 he became enthusiastic about becoming involved with two very different projects. On the one hand was the proposition that he might be interested in joining an expedition to Persia. On the other was the suggestion of applying for a junior post in the Royal Scottish Museum of Natural History. The latter required the undertaking that he would be engaged for several years. He felt, however, that a permanent post would give him professional status and wondered if it might eventually lead to creditable scientific work. It is hard not to see this as a clash between the values and demands of Edwardian middle class Society, in which Ted found himself living, and the Victorian gentlemen adventurers and collectors who were his ancestors and with whose values he was largely brought up. Ted sought advice. No-one else shared Ted's concern about his professional status. In the end conventionality lost out and he did not apply for the post at the Museum. He decided that he had the "wanderlust" too strongly to promise anyone that he would stay put for ten years; life was simply too interesting. The application to join the expedition to Persia, however, faded away under a pile of Grouse feathers as the Inquiry work, rather than finishing as expected, increased to occupy him all year round instead of for just 6 months of the year. This meant that Ted started to fall behind with his other projects. He had taken on too much and whilst he did complete much of the work, it was invariably late and delivered with long apologies. Much of the remainder of 1906 was spent by Ted up in Scotland, tramping grouse moors. He was rarely in one place for any length of time.

It was into this frenzy of work that an unexpected piece of news reached Ted during a study-visit to *Westal* in February 1907. On 11 February Shackleton announced that he was going to lead his own expedition to the Antarctic with the object of reaching the South Pole. The announcement was followed very quickly with a letter on 12 February from Shackleton himself asking Ted to go along as his second in command. Shackleton even suggested that if he was unable to do the Polar journey on account of his health then there was no-one better to do it than Ted - a suggestion that revealed Shackleton himself was still unsure about his health in the southern regions. More importantly, however, Shackleton wanted Ted for his "invaluable" advice. Ory and Ted discussed the subject. She was happy to let him go but getting away from his other commitments was another matter. Ted wrote to Shackleton by return, disappointed that he had to decline his offer on the grounds that he had too many prior commitments to be able to get away, in particular the grouse work, which he was in honour bound to complete. There now followed a frantic exchange of letters between Shackleton, Ted and members of the Grouse Inquiry Board: Ted pledged his loyalty to the Inquiry; Lord Lovat and others thought that Ted's personal qualities made him indispensable to the completion of the work; Shackleton tried to find ways around the problem, even offering to hire an aide and a secretary to speed up the work and so free Ted in time to come along. It was to no avail, Ted could not get away at such short notice. Shackleton thought the resulting decision "almost as bitter a disappointment as when I left *Discovery*"; a stronger indication of the esteem in which Shackleton held Ted could not have been given, indeed Shackleton wrote that if he made it to the Pole, he would still "regret" that Ted was not with him. The influence on polar exploration of the friendship between these two men has never really been considered in any depth but Ted's influence on Shackleton should probably not be underestimated. It seems most unlikely, given Shackleton's strength of feeling and admiration for Ted, that Ted did not have an enormous influence on Shackleton and his future style of leadership. Right down to the departure of Shackleton's ship for the south he was asking Ted's advice on matters and hoping against hope that he would change his mind.

Ted was also, of course, a friend to Captain Scott. On 18 February, when Scott heard that Shackleton was planning an expedition, he contacted Ted as well as Shackleton. It was more or less an open secret amongst *Discovery* officers that Scott wanted to return to finish his work in the Antarctic. It was also more or less known, however, that Scott thought that it was not a practical proposition for him in the short term because of his naval career. In fact, Scott had been secretly preparing expedition plans for some months, he already had the backing of several officers from *Discovery* and he suspected that Shackleton had found out about his plans and was trying to cut across him. Scott wrote asking Shackleton to change his plans and wrote wanting Ted's judgement of the situation (the first that he had heard of Scott's concrete plans). As so often in his life, Ted found himself as the peacemaker as both men turned to him for advice. Any doubts about Shackleton having been given hints of Scott's plans were soon cleared up when Shackleton came to *Westal* to discuss matters with Ted on 4 March. Shackleton assured him that he knew nothing of Scott's plans when he had announced his own and appeared very keen to "do the right thing" in order to clear up their misunderstanding. Indeed, Shackleton appears to have given up the idea of going to McMurdo Sound and using Scott's old *Discovery* huts before his meeting with Ted and without any undue pressure. According to Ted, he simply thought it the right thing to do. Ted thought it the second best thing to do and thought that he should withdraw in the face of Scott's plans and allow Scott to finish what he had started. Ted was far from alone in this view. Indeed, if Ted had been in a position to agree to go with Shackleton at the start it is more than likely that he would in any case have withdrawn at this point. By 31 March Ted had accepted a new invitation from Captain Scott to return with him to the Antarctic, on the clear understanding that he was not available until the end of 1908.

The *Westal* meeting of 4 March cleared the way for Scott and Shackleton to reach an agreement as to their sphere of operations. This was duly drawn up and signed by Shackleton on 17 May, Shackleton agreeing to stay clear of McMurdo Sound. He set sail on *Nimrod* on 30 July with Ted's very best wishes for his success; Ted was nevertheless deeply concerned for Shackleton's health but himself had more pressing worries. At Glasgow station in May he had lost many of his grouse notes when his briefcase was stolen and he had to repeat much of the work.

The years 1906 and 1907 were mostly spent by Ted travelling, often in Scotland to visit grouse moors. He enjoyed these visits, although in keeping with his distaste for big cities, he disliked Edinburgh immensely, where he also carried out much of his work. In September 1907 Ted, Ory and Captain Scott spent some time together with their friends, the Reginald Smiths, at their shooting bungalow at Cortachy, near Kirriemuir. Here they spent the days shooting and making plans for the Antarctic, the closest thing Ted had taken to a holiday in three years. Ted and Scott famously leapt a fence together in pursuit of a Corncrake, and Scott let a roe deer pass through the sights of his gun "because it was so pretty". Ted and Ory also had the use of the hunting lodge the following summer, where they first met Reginald Smith's cousin, Apsley Cherry-Garrard. Ted's frantic work load continued throughout this period. His correspondence alone often took

Otter

him all day to complete. Scott and Ted were rarely out of touch, now, passing ideas between them for the future expedition, in addition to which he was helping a sister with her serious illness and trying to help to sort out Seaman Dell, who was still suffering from an injury sustained aboard *Discovery*. Ted was also involved in the purchasing of a gift "from the Wardroom of the *Discovery* to Captain Scott" on the occasion of his marriage to Kathleen Bruce on 2 September 1908 - not least because of the diplomatic difficulty of whether or not Shackleton, who was still in the Antarctic and who it was now known had broken his agreement with Scott and used McMurdo Sound as his base, should be asked to subscribe.

Wigeon

Shackleton's homecoming on 14 June 1909, having got within 98 miles (176 kms) of the Pole, was hailed as a triumph, Shackleton as a hero. Even Scott put on a brave face in public. Shackleton went on a public lecture tour, lecturing to packed houses in Cheltenham in early December 1909. He was not entertained at *Westal*, although Ted's parents were amongst his audience. To his old friend, Ted, his betrayal was irreconcilable: Shackleton had shown that his word meant so little that nothing he said, and so none of his previous assurances, could be trusted. Shackleton had deliberately chosen to cross Scott - whatever his excuses. In a move very reminiscent of his Cambridge days, Ted broke off his friendship with Shackleton. Shackleton's reaction is unknown but from a person whose opinion he trusted almost above all, it must have been a bitter blow. To a friend Ted wrote:

> ... as for Shackleton I feel the less said the better - I am afraid he has become a regular wrong'un, and I know too much of all that has gone on to speak about him with any pleasure at all. In fact I have broken with him completely and for good, having told him in a somewhat detailed letter exactly what I thought of him and his whole business. I consider he has dragged polar exploration generally in the mud of his own limited and rather low down ambitions - but he will succeed in his aims, of that I have little doubt.

Shackleton's failure to reach the Pole opened the way again for Scott to launch his long planned expedition. With Shackleton's public declaration (made at Ted's specific request) that Scott would cut across no plans of his, Scott's expedition began to gather pace. On 12 July 1909, Ted went to London to meet with Scott, and they discussed Ted becoming the Head of the Scientific Staff. Ted had long since pledged himself to Scott and further hoped that such a senior position would enhance his prospects of a permanent scientific post, preferably in New Zealand, upon his return. He accepted.

Combining his new role on top of his other work, it perhaps seems obvious that something had to give. Having been receiving nothing but unreserved praise for the bird illustrations, and with the deadlines for the pictures having been altered to suit his new circumstances, it was a great shock to Ted on 10 December 1909, to receive a letter terminating the contract for the bird illustrations on the grounds that they were not good enough. In fact, the proposed book was never published. For Ted, it was a great anguish that he was not to be allowed to complete the work closest to his heart. He would, however, complete the work for the Grouse Inquiry. Ted would also complete all of the mammal illustrations for Bell's *A History of British Mammals*. In six years, Ted had hardly had time to draw breath.

Top: L-R Mr and Mrs Reginald Smith, Ory and Captain Scott on a picnic at Cortachy in 1907

Bottom left: Ted c1910   *Bottom right: Oriana c1910*

9. "The Weirdest Bird-Nesting Expedition".

Scott sent a telegram to Ted on 16 September 1909, formally confirming his position as Chief of the Scientific Staff for the forthcoming Polar expedition. The departure date was set for June 1910. On the same day Ted wrote to his father:

> Scott is a man worth working for as a man.- No one can say that it will only have been a Pole-hunt, though that of course is a <u>sine qua non.</u> We must get to the Pole; but we shall get more too... We want the Scientific work to make the bagging of the Pole merely an item in the results.

From early on, Ted was being consulted about many aspects of the expedition and not merely in his own department. He consulted Peary and Borup on the techniques they had used for depot laying in the Arctic. He met Mawson, who wanted to attach his plans to Scott's and be Chief of the Scientific Staff himself - he is perhaps the only person to record that he 'didn't like Wilson'. With the firm Huntley and Palmer, and in consultation with some of his old medical colleagues, Ted developed the biscuits which would be used for sledging rations. He designed the pattern for one of the

Expedition Crest

models of snow goggles which were to be used and which were made by the Cheltenham boot and shoemakers, William Sharpe and Sons. These were proudly displayed in the shop window for the Cheltenham public to see prior to departure. This wasn't to be Cheltenham's only contribution to the expedition. Through Mr Gill, the father of one of the pupils at Cheltenham Ladies' College, where many of Ted's sisters had been pupils, the field telephone was donated which was to be used in making some of the earliest telephone calls in the Antarctic. Financial contributions also came from the town. Scott's second expedition was not a national enterprise, (although the Navy contributed personnel) so he had to raise his own funds, a tiresome task. Many schools up and down the country rallied to the cause, amongst them Ted's old school of Cheltenham College which raised £8.10s (equivalent to £535 today) for a sledge and other equipment; another

Gloucestershire school, Lydney Grammar School in the Forest of Dean, contributed funds towards a pony; and Copthorne, in Sussex, the school at which Ted's brother-in-law was headmaster, also raised the money for a sledge. Thousands of school children up and down the land gave their pocket money to Scott's cause.

Ted's primary responsibility, however, was to select the scientific staff and to obtain all necessary scientific equipment. This he set about doing but it caused him a great deal of worry. He consulted widely to find the best men possible for the job - selection being not only on scientific merit but also on personality. Frank Debenham, who would be selected as one of the geologists when the expedition called at Australia, clinched his place "because of the sparkle in his eye"; the geologist, Wright, and physiographer, Griffith Taylor, were appointed because, on receiving rejection letters, they walked the fifty miles from Cambridge to London in a day, to persuade Ted otherwise. Ted also interceded with Scott on behalf of Apsley Cherry-Garrard, who was eventually accepted on his own account: he would act throughout as Ted's biological assistant. With many other selections besides, and all the preparations and the finalisation of his other projects, Ted was constantly exhausted, taking to painting plates and writing letters standing up so as not to fall asleep. Not withstanding his heavy workload, the full family gathered for a Christmas together at *Westal*. It was the jolliest for many years, with Ted the "life and soul" of the party. As in days gone by, ETW, now nearly 80, starred as Father Christmas, carols were sung and games played. The family graves at Leckhampton Church were visited on Boxing Day. It was to be the last such occasion.

Shortly before he was due to sail for the south, Ted went to Scotland one last time. He had been trying to sail with the whalers from the Shetland Islands for several summers and only now had a chance. He wanted to revise his whales and whaling techniques for the forthcoming scientific work in the south and if possible to attain the services of a Norwegian whaling gunner. There were several unidentified whales and dolphins seen during the *Discovery* expedition and Ted wanted to be able to obtain specimens if possible. He spent several days at sea, witnessing the hunting of whales and making friends with the Norwegian whalers. On his way back to Cheltenham, Ted was still completing mammal and grouse work. He also completed a scientific paper to be read before the Zoological Society of London on his behalf, *The Changes of Plumage in the Red Grouse in Health and in Disease.* Packing in London and *Westal* was frantic and he just made it to Cardiff in time for the farewell Civic Reception.

The expedition ship, *Terra Nova*, sailed from Cardiff on 15 June 1910: bands played, crowds cheered and *Terra Nova* was accompanied on her way by numerous small craft:

The send off from Cardiff was very enthusiastic, enormous crowds having collected at every available spot to cheer and fire guns and detonators, and to make a perfectly hideous din with steam sirens and hooters of which Cardiff seems to possess an infinite number.

Aboard *Terra Nova*, Edward Thomas and Mary Agnes watched it all with the eyes of proud and anxious parents. With Ory they sailed on the ship for some way:

> ...we went out for some 30 miles on the *Terra Nova* and thus had the opportunity of seeing something of the men who were to be Ted's companions in the South - It was a splendid send off, and many friends were there, among them Hodgson (Muggins) of *Discovery* days who would gladly have been of the company. Ted was very bright but fearfully busy - being wanted in every direction as Head of the Scientific Staff. It was sad to say "good bye" when the inevitable tug appeared which was to take us on shore.

Edward Thomas gave Ted a posie of Lemon Verbena from the garden at *Westal*, which Ted dried to remind him of home. It was the last sight of Ted that his parents would ever have. Ory, however, was set to sail with Captain and Mrs Scott by liner to South Africa, Scott having remained behind to try to raise more funds for the expedition.

Ted soon settled down to the regular work routine of an expedition ship. *Terra Nova* sailed to South Africa, via Madeira, where he finished painting the grouse plates, and South Trinidad, where adventurous landings were again made for collecting: Ted coolly sitting on a rock and eating a biscuit as an example to all in a moment of crisis. This time Ted was an old hand, considerably older, in fact, than many aboard but wrote that they were "such a wonderful bunch of men" that "feeling old" soon wore off. He was soon universally known with considerable affection by all, as 'Uncle Bill', or in ruder moments as 'The Director' with various impolite adjectives attached. There were none of the tensions and undercurrents of feeling in the Ward room of *Terra Nova* that there had been on *Discovery*: indeed Ted thought that "almost everyone of the Ward room mess has some exceptional qualities, mental, moral, or physical, or all three" and the atmosphere on board was something akin to an undergraduate outing, with plenty of verbal teasing and ragging. A particular favourite was the game 'Furl Topgallant Sails' which involved ripping each other's shirts off - and sometimes left the combatants without a stitch upon them. Ted enjoyed himself thoroughly and was often in the thick of the action; it let off steam and was good exercise. In between rags were hours of hard labour - four hour shifts stoking the boilers, trimming sails aloft, the sketching of

Madeiran Strorm Petrel

birds, fish and marine invertebrates, the overseeing of the scientific programmes - in particular, the collecting and skinning of birds - and hours of work on the final stages of the Grouse Report; he set up a 'desk' consisting of a wash-stand and a suitcase on which to work. He took little sleep and was always called at 4 a.m. with a mug of thick cocoa.

To Ted's great relief, he was able to post the last of the grouse work home on arrival in South Africa. Ted's contribution to the Grouse Report was an extraordinary accomplishment and Ted felt a great weight lifted from his shoulders. In South Africa too, Ory was waiting for him and they spent his leave visiting the whaling station at Saldanha Bay where Ted supplemented his knowledge of whales. He and Ory were greatly excited by the spectacular birds and flowers which they saw on the way, an 'enchanted paradise' of new sights, smells and colours. Nevertheless, it was here that Ted received a great disappointment. Scott asked him to leave *Terra Nova* and go ahead on a liner to Melbourne to take care of expedition matters such as raising money and appointing geologists. The primary reason for the decision was that Scott wanted time to "get to know his men" and that Ted was the only one who could take his place. Ted thought that the decision would be open to mis-interpretation, as did Lieutenant Evans (Second in Command). On a more personal level, Ted had been loving ship-board life, loathed raising money, hated official functions and didn't relish the prospect of looking after the expedition wives in the shape of his own, Mrs Scott and Mrs Evans. Nevertheless, he went, the extra weeks spent with Ory bringing some compensation. His journey aboard *R.M.S Corinthic* to Hobart and from there to Sydney by ferry and train, was something of a chore. He did not get on well with Kathleen Scott, although they tolerated one another. She thought him 'humourless' and disliked being treated as an expedition 'outsider', a sign that she was probably jealous. He almost certainly found her pagan hedonism distasteful and didn't fall in love with her, a reaction she expected from most men. She made demands on him which he thought were out of order, the worst being to set sail at night, with the wives and a bag of mail, in a rough sea, to greet *Terra Nova* the moment she sailed into Melbourne. Ted dryly wrote that:

> ...in future I hope it will never fall to my lot to have more than one wife at a time to look after, at any rate in a motor launch , in a running sea at night time.

Tawny Frogmouth

A relieved Ted handed over the wives and the money raising; the money they needed to raise in Australia was eventually donated and they sailed for New Zealand in good spirits. This was despite the fact that Scott had received a telegram from the Norwegian explorer Roald Amundsen, "Beg leave inform you proceeding Antarctic. Amundsen". It was a deliberately vague telegram. It was generally thought on board that he would be heading for the Weddell Sea; he certainly wasn't considered a threat to the objectives of the expedition. Amundsen himself, having publicly maintained that he was leading a scientific expedition to study the Arctic Ocean ice cap but hoping to reach the North Pole, whilst not engaging in a 'Polar race', had kept his plans hidden even from his crew until Madeira, and then secretly sailed for the Ross Sea, his sole object to beat Scott to the South Pole. The media slowly woke up to what was occurring and began to create the myth of 'the race for the South Pole', a race which Scott and the *Terra Nova* Expedition team did not , even as they politely fielded questions in New Zealand, understand was happening; indeed, the first inkling Scott had that Amundsen might be heading for the Pole was from the direction of media questions and he still thought that Amundsen intended to attempt it from the Weddell Sea.

Once again in Lyttelton, Ted and Ory renewed their New Zealand friendships. Ted discussed the possibility of entering the priesthood upon his return from the south with his old friend the Bishop of Wellington, an idea which he gave up relatively soon, however. His struggles with Truth and how to instantiate it through his own life and actions were as strong as ever. A general mixture of work and pleasure filled Ted and Ory's days with one exception: Mrs Evans and Mrs Scott had an enormous row, in which Ory became involved. The crew of *Terra Nova* might have been notable for its generally good relationships but this was not to be true of the wives. Nevertheless, Ory was far too tough to be intimidated and she and Ted passed happy days until they took the train to Dunedin to rejoin the ship, which had sailed a few days before.

Terra Nova sailed from Port Chalmers on Tuesday 29 November 1910 amidst cheering crowds and small craft. Ory was aboard for as long as possible, until she had to leave, waving for all she was worth from the deck of the tug until Ted was once again out of sight and heading for the unknown. They would never see each other again.

Ted once again sailed into the great Southern Ocean. *Terra Nova* was so heavily laden that when she hit a fierce storm on her way south she nearly sank, the entire ship's company turning out to bail for hour upon endless hour. Ted never doubted that they would pull through after his eyes picked out a rainbow at the height of the storm, a sign which gave him heart, he in turn keeping up the hearts of others. They took it in turns to snatch a nap in the few remaining dry bunks. On 9 December they entered the pack ice, which detained them for three weeks. Ted was not unhappy as it gave him and the scientific staff ample opportunity to study its wildlife and to paint its splendours.

> The sunlight at midnight in the pack is perfectly wonderful. One looks out upon endless fields of broken ice, all violet and purple in the low shadows, and all gold and orange and rose-red on the broken edges which catch the light, while the sky is emerald green and salmon pink, and these two beautiful tints are reflected in the pools of absolutely still water which here and there lie between the ice floes.

Now and again one hears a penguin cry out in the stillness... only intensifying the wonderful stillness and beauty of the whole fairy-like scene...

It was, however, an unhelpful and ultimately fatal delay to expedition plans. Ted spent much of his time in the crow's nest sketching and watching. His fellow crew members were to be shaken many years later when they discovered that he had also used it as a private chapel, going there with regularity to meditate and pray; none of them knew. When they finally reached Cape Crozier, where Scott and Ted had hoped that they would be able to build their base, the swell was too great to make a landing and so they again sailed into McMurdo Sound, choosing to make their home at a point called the Skuary and renamed Cape Evans by Scott, in honour of his Second-in-Command. The business of unloading and of building their hut was commenced at once and completed in a week.

Adelie Penguins

Within days, on 24 January 1911, Scott led a journey to the south using both dogs and ponies in order to lay depots of supplies for the Polar journey the following season. The start had been badly delayed by their time in the pack ice. Ted was one of the dog drivers. They headed south over the Barrier averaging 10 or 11 miles (18 to 20 kms) per day. Delayed further by blizzards and with decreasing temperatures as the sledging season drew towards a close, Scott left his major supply depot on 17 February, at 79° 281/2' South, 30 miles (55 kms) short of the 80th parallel where he had hoped to leave One Ton Depot. It was to prove a fatal shortfall. The ponies did not do as well as had been hoped, sinking in the soft snow. Two died from exhaustion. The dogs did not perform well either, their diet was insufficient and they under-performed. Although this was later corrected, it confirmed Scott's mistrust of dogs, which originated from his *Discovery* experiences.

On their return to 'Safety Camp', their base on the edge of the Barrier, they spent some time waiting for the sea ice to form to allow their return to the old *Discovery* hut at Hut Point. They were difficult days. Scott had received mail on his return informing him that *Terra Nova* had found Amundsen, a small group of men and over 100 dogs camped at the Bay of Whales, an inlet in the Great Ice Barrier. He wasn't in the Weddell Sea at all, in Antarctic terms he was just next door. It was a bitter blow. Ted thought that Amundsen's choice of base was unsafe but that if he survived the winter, he would travel faster to the Pole with his dogs than they could. There was anxious worry and debate about the implications of the news.

The journey back to Hut Point was a catalogue of miscommunication, mistakes and courage in the face of them. Men and ponies ended up drifting out on breaking up sea ice, surrounded by Killer Whales. The result was that whilst all the men reached the hut safely, few of the ponies did. So far Scott had lost two ponies and two dogs in the storm at sea, one motor tractor through the sea ice during unloading, and six ponies on the depot laying journey. He started to become concerned. Ted was not. For him it was all a part of Divine purpose and the seeming randomness of mistakes and miscommunication was all part of their education.

The days at Hut Point were remembered fondly by those who were there. Captain Oates, of the 6th Inniskilling Dragoons, was a great clown and his attempts to persuade Ted to part with the medicinal brandy in the first aid box kept them all amused. Nevertheless, it was with thankfulness that they returned to Cape Evans in April. They soon settled into a regular winter routine. Ted generally started his day with a snow bath, often with Bowers. 'Birdie' Bowers had much in common with Ted. His exceptional working abilities and jolly personality had led to his unanticipated selection for the shore party. Underneath it all, he possessed a similar strong faith. In addition to sharing an icy bath, they also regularly walked up 'the Ramp' together to read the temperature at the outlying meteorological stations. Ted also kept the extensive scientific programme going, worked up his sketches, illustrated a new edition of the *South Polar Times* and was the confidante of almost all. Many of Ted's wider contributions to expedition life were made possible through having a biological assistant in the form of Cherry-Garrard. He was proving to be a godsend to Ted in helping to ease some of the more time consuming basic biological work, such as skinning specimens. Despite being very short-sighted he had also proved himself as a sledger of remarkable toughness.

In the confined atmosphere of the hut everyone worked hard; there was also a great deal of verbal teasing, in the place of ragging (which was banned in the hut), the laconic Oates being a particular master. Oates' dry, slightly supercilious personality was in its element amongst his companions, many of whom gave him as good as they got. Ted too, could banter with the best when he put his mind to it, on one occasion retorting to Oates, "The way thoughts flash through your mind, Titus, reminds me of a snail's climbing a cabbage stalk". It must have been a good riposte as it was remembered many years later. Ted, however, had more on his mind than verbal sparring. He had something very special in store for the winter scientific programme.

At 11am on 27 June 1911 carrying 757lbs (343 kgs) of equipment on 2 sledges, Ted, Birdie Bowers and Apsley Cherry-Garrard left the hut at Cape Evans on one of the most extraordinary polar journeys ever undertaken. It had become necessary because they had been unable to establish the wintering base at Cape Crozier and so they now became involved in a 130 mile (240 km) trek from Cape Evans to Cape Crozier and back, in the winter darkness. Ted called it "the weirdest bird-nesting expedition that has been or ever will be" and its aim was to make one of the biggest scientific breakthroughs of the 20th century, by proving the link between dinosaurs and birds. It was a general scientific belief of the time that ontogony recapitulated phylogeny, that is, that the individual embryo of a developing organism passed through every stage of its' species' evolution. It was also thought that the Emperor Penguin, belonging to one of the oldest known forms of fossil bird at that time, was a particularly primitive bird and that if there was a link between dinosaurs and birds that it was most likely to be found, therefore, in the early embryonic stages of this species. Ted particularly wanted to find vestiges of teeth and to test theories connecting feathers with reptilian scales. The possibility of making this important scientific breakthrough therefore required visiting the Emperor Penguins soon after they had laid their eggs. On the previous *Discovery* expedition, Ted had concluded that the Emperor Penguin must lay and incubate their eggs in the middle of the Antarctic winter and so there was nothing else for it but a winter journey. Scott appears to have made the promise to Ted before they left England that he would be allowed to complete this aspect of his personal scientific work, although he tried to dissuade him from going. Ted nevertheless persisted and promised to bring everyone back alive. So it was that the three men walked into the frozen world outside the hut in search of the egg of the Emperor Penguin. In addition to going bird-nesting, Ted, Bowers and Cherry-Garrard had also agreed to experiment with different types of sledging rations, each consuming different quantities of fat, carbohydrate, etc. to ensure the best possible sledging ration for the Polar journey later in the year. Amongst their supplies, therefore, was a mixture of foodstuffs to last them for six weeks.

Emperor Penguin

The average temperature on this journey was -60°F (-51°C); it fell as low as -77°F (-60°C). It was so cold that their teeth cracked. The pus inside their blistered frostbite froze. Their sleeping bags became solid and could not be rolled up - it took two men to beat them back into shape for the third man to enter, each time they rested. It took them four hours to dress and break camp. It was so cold that within seconds of leaving their tent in the morning their outer garments were frozen, trapping the men inside into the same armoured posture for the day. Cherry-Garrard had to spend four hours sledging looking up at the stars because he had made the mistake of admiring them on leaving the tent one morning. They made their way gingerly through the darkness, negotiating huge ice pressure ridges, along the length of Ross Island to Cape Crozier. Here they built a camp consisting of their tent and a small stone igloo which Ted named 'Oriana Hut' in honour of their wedding anniversary. They then proceeded onto the ice and were the first men ever to see the Emperor Penguin brooding its eggs. Collecting five eggs, and killing three adult birds for blubber for their stove, they returned to their camp, breaking two of the eggs on the way. They planned to return to collect more but were soon caught up in a world of swirling drift as a blizzard hit them with a ferocious intensity. Ted spent the night in agony as a drop of penguin blubber had spat into his eye and he thought that he had lost the sight in it. Worse was to come. The following day, their tent blew away in the storm and was shortly followed by the roof of their igloo and a good portion of their equipment. It was Ted's 39th birthday - Bowers had brought a tin of sweets to celebrate. Each man lay in his sleeping bag exposed to the ferocity of an Antarctic blizzard. They sang hymns, said prayers and occasionally checked if the others still lived. Many hours later, when the blizzard had all but ceased, they emerged to take stock of their seemingly impossible position. They wandered around the camp and quite miraculously found their tent only a short distance away. Bowers wanted to go for more eggs but Ted ordered them home. Every time they camped, Bowers tied himself to the tent so that it wouldn't get away without him again. The homeward leg was a nightmare of cold, exposure and grim determination but they kept their senses of humour and still remembered to say 'please' and 'thankyou' each to the other. As they approached Cape Evans, Ted turned to his companions and quietly said,

> I want to thank you two for what you have done. I couldn't have found two better companions - and what is more I never shall.

They arrived back at the hut at 10pm on 1 August. Ted was disappointed not to have seen more of the penguins but the bird-nesting had been a success. They had acquired the eggs of the Emperor Penguin and would be able to test important scientific hypotheses through their examination. Further than this, they had survived the Antarctic winter and for six weeks had continuously experienced some of the lowest temperatures ever endured by human beings. With the accumulation of ice, their clothing weighed 66lbs (30kgs) more than when they had left the hut; they had to be levered out of it. Sleeping bags that had weighed 18lbs (8kgs) now weighed 45lbs (20kgs). The photographer, Herbert Ponting, standing in awe with his colleagues as the accomplishment of the three men sunk in, took their picture. He wrote that the looks on their faces haunted him for days.

Diagram of 'Oriana Hut'

- 90 -

*Three Men stumbling
in a blizzard*

Top: Ted's last Christmas at Westal December 1909, Family Group
Back Row: L-R Elsie; Bernard R; Jim; Norah; Ted;
Front Row: L-R Lily (with Tony); Ida; Bernard; Mary Agnes; Godfrey R. (With Ruth); ETW; Ory; Polly (with Peter)
Left: "Final Directions" Ted and Ory
Bottom left: Getting to know the dogs
Bottom right: The last informal picture of Ted in the Wilson family albums, labelled "Last Word, Fit and Happy"

Top: L-R Bowers; Ted and Cherry-Garrard leaving the hut at Cape Evans on the Winter
Journey to Cape Crozier
Bottom: L-R Ted; Bowers and Cherry-Garrard on their return to the hut at Cape Evans
from the Winter Jouney to Cape Crozier, the Photographer, Ponting, said that their
looks 'haunted' him for days

10. "All is Well."

The effects of the Winter Journey to Cape Crozier lasted for several weeks. It took time for the circulation to restore feeling to the tips of fingers and toes that had been numb for a month. Ted nevertheless recommenced his early morning snow baths with Bowers within two days of getting back. He also returned to the daily climbs up the Ramp to take observations and began to paint again, adding picture after stunning picture, completing around 100. He also worked on the Scientific Report to be sent back with the relief ship. He was extremely pleased with the progress that the scientific staff had made, the expedition was well on course to making "bagging the Pole merely an item in the results". He was admired in turn by his staff who would 'hover' around him hoping to earn his approval for a piece of work; indeed, all of the officers hoped for compliments on their work from 'Uncle Bill'. They sought his advice on any difficulties that they were having in work and on the personal level. He in turn, looked after each of them with tender loving care and would stop whatever he was doing to attend to whomsoever it was who sought his help or advice. Ted was particularly concerned for Oates at the start of Antarctic spring sledging. This entailed dozens of minor forays with the ponies to get men and beasts into peak condition for the long journey ahead. The training didn't always go according to plan: on one occasion even Ted ended up running three miles (5.5 kms)over the ice to recover his bolted pony. It created plenty of worry and tension. Ted wrote:

Man leading a pony and sledge

> I am very anxious about Titus Oates, who has had a great string of rotten unsound ponies thrown on his hands, and who is spoken to rather as though he was to blame whenever anything goes wrong with them, and of course he doesn't like it.

Ted was pleased, however, to have such a competent man as Oates looking after the ponies, as was Scott; but Scott was under immense pressure during this period and often let his frustration show. Ted and Scott handled their intense feelings in very different ways, though they implicitly understood each other's deep sensitivities. This was, perhaps, the basis of their immense mutual respect, which deepened further as the expedition progressed. Scott thought that Ted was the cleverest man of the group, his tact, breadth of knowledge and unselfishness making him something akin to "an Oracle". Ted thought that Scott was the cleverest all round intellect that he had ever met. Indeed, many of their companions had similar ideas, thinking of Scott as a frustrated scientist because his general grasp of, and interest in, their diverse work was immense. Whilst many of them "stood in awe" of Scott, however, they "loved" Ted, indeed, Cherry-Garrard thought that it was almost impossible to merely "like" him. Ted himself would have been quite astonished to hear of the depth of his companions' widespread esteem.

At the end of October, as the days for their departure on the Polar Journey drew closer, the tension in the hut quite naturally rose. The doubts which always accompanied Ted as a part of his struggle with Truth, on this occasion doubts about whether he was really needed on the expedition at all, evaporated under a flood of those seeking his counsel. Just before he left the hut, Ted wrote to Ory:

> ...I have been having talks with several people, and hearing grievances and confidences. It is a great thing to know that one has had a job to do and that one has been doing it more or less unconsciously and that to some extent it has come off...my goodness! I had hours of it yesterday; as though I was a bucket it was poured into me... Grievances there are bound to be and disagreements, but as long as everyone can keep them from boiling over I think we can rightly say that we have been extraordinarily free from any want of unity...

Ted's companions were sure that it was due to him that the peace was largely kept.

Leading the pony 'Nobby', on 1 November 1911 Ted left the relative comfort of the hut at Cape Evans with the main pony group of the Southern Party. The two slow motor tractors had left Cape Evans with their supplies on 24 October, the dog teams would leave a few days later. The eventual destination for a small party of the men would be the South Pole. Scott had, much to his credit, decided not to alter his plans in the knowledge of Amundsen's appearance and so not to race for the Pole, although he and many of his companions still hoped that an act of Providence might mean that they would indeed be the first to attain it. This meant that the Norwegians only would be 'racing'. In fact, Scott postponed his first announced departure date slightly in the hope that the weather would have improved for the ponies. In the face of all the anxieties, Ted was sure in himself that he had come down here "for a purpose" and should see it through, rather than worry or withdraw because of any concerns over what "might happen". The send off from the hut was accompanied with ringing cheers and photographs were taken with sledge flags flying. Then it was on to the tough business of Antarctic travel and a proposed journey of 1532 miles (2837 kms) to the Pole and back, all on foot.

The weather on the Barrier was not good. Temperatures were often below 0°F (-17°C) and almost constant snow falls were interspersed with a grey and damp

haze. The snow fall caused the going to be tough on the ponies, which sank to their fetlocks. They only managed 10 to 12 miles (18 to 22 kms) per day, reaching One Ton Depot after 15 days. The motor tractors had not even managed to get that far, the motor-party man-hauled the supplies instead, so as not to jeopardise the Polar journey. Scott, however, was sure that the day would come when beasts were replaced by machines and the immorality of using animals to do haulage in the Antarctic would be over. They left depots approximately every 70 miles (130 kms), each stage accompanied by the constant worry as to whether the ponies would endure the difficult conditions. Ted noted,

Scott (RFS), Oates (TO) and Bowers (B) leading ponies over the Great Ice Barrier

"Much depends on what the ponies do during the next 14 days, by which time we shall be at the foot of the Beardmore Glacier". In fact, it was the weather that did not do as expected. 12 miles (22 kms) from the foot of the Beardmore Glacier, the temperature rose to +35.5°F (+2°C) and a blizzard of wet snow kept them trapped in their sopping tents and sleeping bags for four days, the howling drift reaching nearly to the peak of their tents. It was the fifth blizzard encountered after Cape Evans but by far the worst, causing serious delay. When they were able to continue, the ponies sank up to their bellies on the march so it was decided to end their suffering. The weaker animals had been shot to feed to the dogs during the journey across the Barrier but five animals were shot at the end and added to the cache of supplies at 'Shambles Camp', including 'Nobby'. Ted had fed his ration of biscuits to 'Nobby' during the final march. Everyone was glad that the ordeal of the ponies was over. Ted led the congratulations to Titus Oates on a job well done: the ponies had achieved all that had been expected of them, if a little slower than desired, and reached to within sight of the snout of the Beardmore Glacier. They had performed better than the dogs of 1902-03, reaching further South. This time, however, the dog food was much improved and the two expedition dog teams travelled very easily to the Beardmore Glacier. From here, however, Scott sent the two teams home. He wanted to preserve them for the next season's series of sledging journeys, considering the scientific work which they were planning to conduct more important than the Polar journey. From now on, it was man-hauling all the way. The men, who pulled 200lbs (90kgs) each in the traces, preferred it that way, regarding pulling the sledges themselves as honest work, better than watching animals suffer.

The Beardmore Glacier is one of the longest glaciers in the world. It is over 100 miles (180 kms) long, up to 40 miles (74 kms) wide and rises to 10,000 feet (3,000m) above sea-level. Parts of it are heavily crevassed, one factor in Scott's decision not to risk bringing animals up it. Shackleton, its discoverer, had experienced a surface of hard blue ice over which to travel. The recent blizzard, however, had covered the lower reaches with soft snow into which the travellers sank to their knees. Everyone's lips were cracked and bleeding from exposure to the wind and sun, the sledges often overturned or got stuck, and snow blindness was a regular occurrence; Ted continued sketching all the way. The party only advanced short distances daily. Once they rose high enough to encounter an icy surface, they progressed at nearer to 20 miles (37 kms) per day. They established the 'Upper Glacier Depot' at around 7,000 feet (2120m) where the second supporting party of four men was sent home. Eight men continued to climb, falling into crevasses but making remarkable progress, 14 to 17 miles (26 to 32 km) daily, when their calculations had called for 10 (18). Christmas was celebrated with extra rations. On New Years Eve the worn runners on the sledges were replaced. It was during this operation that Petty Officer Evans cut his hand on the metal runners which had been sharpened by travel over the hard ice - but, thinking it insignificant, he said nothing.

The five man sledging team

On 3 January, 169 miles (313 km) from the Pole, Scott sent back the third and last supporting party. In a decision that has been much criticised, Scott decided to take five men to the Pole rather than four: himself, Ted, Bowers, Oates and P.O. Evans. It meant a certain amount of re-organisation and whilst unplanned (all the supplies were packed in units of four) it was probably not as impulsive as some have suggested. Significantly, before he left the hut, Ted had sketched a party man-hauling a sledge but with five men rather than the usual four. Ted was not prone to imaginative pictures, aiming to depict accurately the truth through art (although it should be noted that this did not always mean depicting everything as seen). Frank Debenham, who was one of those who had been close to Ted on this expedition, thought that this picture was very probably an indication that Scott had mentioned the possibility of taking five men to Ted quite early. It is equally possible that Ted had another premonition. Nothing is mentioned and so we will never be sure but it is certainly a sketch to arouse interest. At any event, the decision to take five men is a sign of the strength of their position at this time. It did not make the Polar party short of food in itself and gave them an extra man to help pull, so that they would cover the distance between the depots faster. If it had an adverse affect, it was that it took longer to cook meals for five and reduced tent space, making it more uncomfortable; by removing a man from the supporting party it also gave them a tougher return journey. Lieutenant Evans was sent back with Petty Officers Lashly and Crean; they would be awarded the Albert Medal for their bravery in saving Evans' life when he succumbed to scurvy. When the supporting party turned back, the Polar party was in a good position and full of optimism.

Within a few days, the optimism was tempered. Evans' hand needed treatment: the cut was full of pus and required regular attention from Ted. They were delayed for another day by a blizzard. As they hauled across the last miles to the Pole they experienced a difficult pulling surface covered with ice crystals which clogged the sledge runners and slowed their nevertheless extraordinary progress. Ted thought that the crystals on the runners looked like gorse. The temperatures which they faced on the Polar Plateau were also low, falling to -27°F (-33°C). In their diaries there are the first signs of fatigue and starting to feel the cold. They were often iced up during the march. On 16 January, a short distance from the Pole, signs of Norwegian cairns, tracks and camps were seen. They were not, after all, to be the first to the South Pole. Amundsen, with his knowledge of Scott's plans ensured a head start, had travelled with dogs and encountering very little in the way of bad weather or delays had arrived five weeks before and was, in fact, almost back at his ship. Ted took the news with his usual equanimity. Whilst he thought it a great honour and was pleased to have been chosen for the Polar party his desire to reach the Pole was probably the least strong amongst the five men. He was at least as keen to get back to Hut Point to receive his mail, with all its news of Ory, of the home folks at *Westal* and the publication of his previous five years of work. For him, as with all things, the Polar journey and its success or failure was a part of the Will of God in which he had been called upon to play his part. For Ted too, honest striving, the sincerity of motive and action, were what was important, not worldly success. Ted was no doubt a very calming influence when they "discussed things" in the tent that evening.

They camped at the Pole on 17 January 1912. The wind was blowing at force 4 to 6 all day, in a temperature of -22°F (-30°C), Ted thought it a "bitter" day. With the wind chill it is unsurprising that Oates, Evans and Bowers all suffered from "pretty severe frost bite". Ted thought with the others that Amundsen hadn't quite hit the right spot for the Pole...

> ... but in any case are all agreed that he can claim prior right to the Pole itself. He has beaten us in so far as he made a race of it. We have done what we came for all the same and as our programme was made out.

The 18th brought similar conditions. They explored the area and found the spot which, from their measurements, they best judged to be the South Pole itself. Here, they 'flew the Union Jack and all their own flags', taking their photographs by using a piece of string to release the shutter. They found a tent left by the Norwegians not far away and in it a note from Amundsen, asking Scott to carry a letter to the King of Norway. Ted took a spirit lamp "which I have wanted for sterilising and making disinfectant lotions of snow." Evans' infected hand was still requiring regular treatment. Ted made some quick sketches. None of them was unhappy to turn to the north, which they did, under the circumstances, in good spirits. The return journey now became a race to try to get back to the ship before it departed again from the Antarctic.

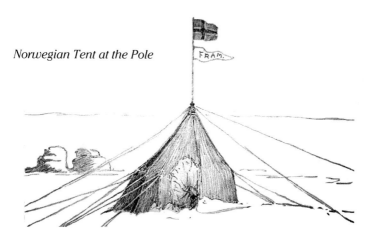

Norwegian Tent at the Pole

They started off well, making good distances in low temperatures over difficult pulling surfaces. Ted described them once again with the vivid imagery of his Cotswold home:

> The surface was very largely eggshell porcelain, white and glistening like a woodpecker's egg and as thin - almost always gives way under foot. [In] some places there are 6 or 7 thin crusts in 2 or 3 inches depth of this snow.

With the sheer exertion of pulling, they were tiring; they endured frostbite in the low temperatures; they suffered from snow blindness through removing their goggles to follow more efficiently their old trail; Ted strained a tendon in his leg; Oates felt the cold more than the others and his frost-bitten toes were turning black; Scott fell and injured his shoulder; little things that suggest that they were becoming exhausted. Evans, however, was taking it badly. He had frozen the tips of his fingers. These too, soon started to suppurate, and he shed two of his nails. He started to get angry with himself and his morale started to slip: with his hands being relatively useless and unable to do camp work it seems certain that he felt that he was letting his companions down. On 4 February Evans fell twice, the second fall into a shallow crevasse with Scott, after which Scott first noted him as being "dull and incapable on the march".

They were glad to be back onto the Beardmore Glacier. On 8 and 9 February they took part of the day off from marching to geologise around the base of Mt.

Buckley, where Shackleton had found pieces of coal. This was not only a much needed rest and morale booster; Ted made detailed geological notes. They collected 35lbs (16kgs) of geological specimens in all, as they went along the glacier, which were amongst the most important scientific finds of the entire expedition. Ted recognised the importance to science of the fossilised plants which he found but he would never know just how valuable they were.

They had a difficult time descending the glacier, getting lost in ice ridges and crevasses and only just finding their depot of provisions before they ran completely out of supplies. They were tiring more and more and not covering the distances required in time. In part this was due to Evans who was visibly weakening. They reduced rations. They were near to the Pillar Rock at the bottom of the Beardmore Glacier when Evans collapsed on 16 February. Ted thought that:

HRB.

Bowers

> Evans collapse has much to do with the fact that he has never been sick in his life and is now helpless with his hands frost-bitten.

This, of course, was written for Ory and the family and would have meant a great deal to his mother in the context of their correspondence during Ted's St. George's days about "the teaching power of sickness". Ted had been nursing Evans for weeks and clearly thought his collapse had an important psychological, as well as physical, aspect. The following day Evans resumed pulling the sledge but stopped to adjust his footwear. His colleagues found him finally collapsed when they went back to find him. Ted thought that he had "injured his brain" in one of his many falls. He died that evening.

After a few hours, the four remaining men continued on their way and were soon feasting on pony meat at Shambles Camp. Back on the Barrier supplies were expected to be plentiful again. The temperatures which they faced, however, were unusually low, often down to -40°F (-40°C) and sometimes below. It was, therefore, a serious blow to find that each of their depots contained a shortage of oil, which they relied upon to melt drinking water and to cook. The paraffin appeared to have leaked or evaporated from the sealed containers. Morale was constantly being knocked; they kept going through grim determination. Ted stopped writing his diary on 28 February. He had kept a diary for most of his life, he believed in recording how he spent his time to ensure that he spent it well, it was a central part of his ascetic and spiritual life. To stop writing it could only mean that there was something of greater spiritual importance demanding his time: the sacrifice of self in the service of others. The ideal that he had first envisioned at Cambridge was becoming a reality. On 2 March as well as finding a shortage of oil at another depot, Oates disclosed his blackened, frost-bitten feet. Gangrene was apparently starting to set in. With cold temperatures, fatigue, a bad pulling surface and either no wind or wind from the north so that they could hoist no sail, it was clear that they were in a serious position. His companions forced Ted to hand over the opium tablets from the medical kit so that they could choose to end their lives, if they so wished. Ted, in doing his best to nurse Oates, started to suffer himself, getting more serious frostbite but Scott recorded that Ted and Bowers were "unendingly cheerful". Both of these men had a very profound faith which kept them going. Ted found great inspiration in the small books that he had taken with him to read, a book of Tennysons' poems, a New Testament and prayer book and a book of Rutherford's *Letters* lent to him by his mother. In the latter are written the margin notes that show Ted wrestling with the events around him. Next to the passage "Suffering is

Oates

the badge that Christ hath put upon his followers" is the poignant remark "May God grant this true" and in an entry dated 12 March 1912 he underlined the passage

> If your Lord take any of them home to His house, before the storm come on, take it well... Make a surrender of those that are gone, and of those that are yet alive to Him.

They staggered on as best as they could. Oates must have been in severe pain. On 16 or 17 March he could take no more. In an effort to save his companions Oates walked out of the tent and into a blizzard saying "I am just going outside and may be some time". Ted thought that Oates had shown very great courage in his suffering and had died a noble death.

It was not enough. Scott, Ted and Bowers marched on for three more days. Scott's feet were now badly frost-bitten, the best he could hope for was amputation. They deposited some of their heavier equipment but at Ted's special request continued to carry the geological specimens. 11 miles (20 kms) from the major supply cache at One Ton Depot they were again hit by a blizzard. The three companions lay in their tent and finished their fuel, whilst the blizzard raged around them. After laying up for a day or two, Ted and Bowers intended to make a dash for supplies and to bring food and fuel back to Scott. The weather never cleared enough for them to attempt it. The blizzard lasted for at least nine days more; how long precisely is unknown. They decided to die a natural death. Somehow, as they lay so close to reaching their abundant supplies, slowly starving and freezing to death - quite literally - they found the strength to write their last letters. Scott wrote his famous "Message to the Public" asking that their dependants be cared for. In his letter to Ory he noted that Ted was sacrificing himself to the needs of others even at the end. As the screaming blizzard raged outside, Ted tried to write letters to all his family members and closest friends but it was to Ory that he wrote at length, his eyes filled with what Scott called their "comfortable blue look of hope" shining through his final words to the woman he loved.

To my most beloved Wife. God be with you in your troubles dear, when I am gone ... I have written another short letter to you which is stowed in one of your canvas satchels with my diary (Borroughs Wellcome's diary) and two Piers sketchbooks... I leave this life in absolute faith and happy belief that we shall merely know nothing till we are together again and if God wishes you to wait long without me it will be to some good purpose - all is for the best to those who love God - and oh my Ory we have both loved Him with our whole lives - all is well. I have no fear or horror of death for God is very near us both. Bless you my own dear wife - take heart and live your life out. We have struggled to the end and we have nothing to regret our whole journey record is clean - and Scott's diary gives the account. Two of the five of us are dead. The rest of us are fit to go on, only God seems to wish otherwise as he has given us quite impossible weather and we are now clean run out of food and fuel after a long period of very short fuel and intense cold and headwinds. The barrier has beaten us though we got to the Pole. Our record is clear. It is God's will and all is for the best. We have struggled against very heavy odds to the bitter end. I have had a very happy life and I look forward to a very happy life hereafter when we shall all be together again... these are small things - life itself is a small thing to me now... I am going to spend the remainder of my time here reading your small testament and prayer book - I do not cease to pray for you and to desire that you may be filled with the knowledge of His will - strengthened with Grace by His infinite power into all patience and with long suffering and joyfulness. Giving thanks unto the Father - God be with you - my own dear wife - with joyfulness - I am quite happy and with no fear of death at all - and I feel it is within a day's reach now at the most - I trust God to comfort you and the dear old Dad and Mother and all our home folks - may he comfort all who will be unhappy mainly on your account - let them have no unhappiness about me. God knows I am sorry to be the cause of sorrow to anyone in the world but everyone must die - and at every death there must be some sorrow... all the things I had hoped to do with you after this expedition are as nothing now - but there are greater things in store for us to do in the world to come - and God joins us together - we shall certainly meet again. I have thought much of the dear Reginald Smiths - they are like us deeply in love with one another - and I simply love them both - I would like to have got within reach of their letters and yours before going out - but God will let me know all about that if it really matters... don't imagine me dying in any pain or suffering or in sorrow - either bodily or mental - for I shall simply fall asleep and awake with Christ - my only great regret is in leaving you to struggle through your life alone -

but God may have even now closed yours before mine and I may be coming to you by a quicker way - I feel so happy now in having got time to write to you - one of my notes will surely reach you - My sledge flag and the keys to the sledge flag are wrapped up in a black flag with a note of Amundsen's which I brought from the Pole - they will be in the gear collected from our last camp, and I am leaving a note to the commander of the expedition to see that these things and all my gear at the hut go to you - you will be able to get my things from New Zealand. The dear Bowens have some and others are at the tourist bureau... your little books... will be in my hand or in my breast pocket whenever the end comes - I have the little silver crucifix tied to the Holland cover - your photos are in these books - they have been well used and a very great joy to me... there is nothing else of use on me - Dad's little compass and mother's little comb and looking glass are in my pocket - all is well dear...

The tent as found in November 1912

Top:
Captain Scott and the Southern Party,
28 November 1911. Ted is sitting on the sledge in front of Bowers
Bottom:
L-R Evans; Bowers; Ted and Scott eating Hoosh in their tent

Top:
Scott; Ted; Oates and Evans pulling for
the Pole (photo by Bowers)

Middle:
Ted and Nobby

Bottom:
At the Pole, 18 January 1912,
L-R Ted; Bowers (Pulling the string);
Evans; Scott and Oates

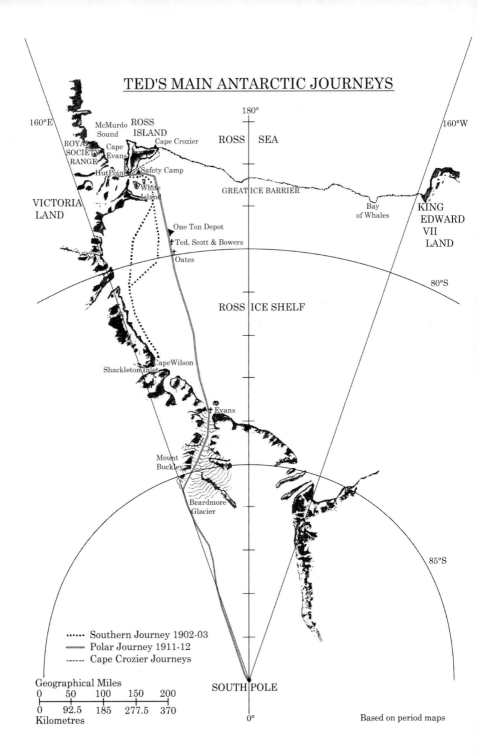

TED'S MAIN ANTARCTIC JOURNEYS

160°E

McMurdo
Sound

ROSS
ISLAND

Cape Crozier

ROSS   SEA

160°W

ROYAL
SOCIETY
RANGE

Cape
Evans

HutPoint   Safety Camp

White
Island

GREAT ICE BARRIER

Bay
of Whales

KING
EDWARD
VII
LAND

VICTORIA
LAND

One Ton Depot

Ted, Scott & Bowers

Oates

80°S

ROSS ICE SHELF

CapeWilson

Shackleton Inlet

Evans

Mount
Buckley

Beardmore
Glacier

85°S

····· Southern Journey 1902-03
——— Polar Journey 1911-12
----- Cape Crozier Journeys

Geographical Miles
0   50   100   150   200

0   92.5   185   277.5 370
Kilometres

SOUTH POLE

0°

Based on period maps

11. "Cheltenham's Antarctic Hero"

*****

It's not what happens to you,
it's what you make of it that matters.

EAW

*****

On 12 November 1912 a search party led by the expedition Surgeon, Dr. Atkinson, discovered the bodies of Ted, Scott and Bowers in the tent. All the members of the party were deeply moved by what they saw: Ted, half reclining and sitting facing the door of the tent wrapped in his sleeping bag, his arms crossed over his chest, with a gentle smile on his face, looking for all the world as if he was about to wake up; Bowers toggled up in his bag; and Scott, lying with his arm thrust out of his bag towards Ted. Their bodies showed signs of their ordeal. After a brief examination, their diaries, personal belongings and the geological specimens were collected. Ted's small New Testament was left with his body; Atkinson read the burial service; they sang Onward Christian Soldiers and collapsed the tent over them as they lay. Above them they built a great cairn of snow surmounted with a cross of skis and they were left to lie in the peace of the Antarctic. The bodies of Oates and Evans were never found. On Observation Hill a wooden memorial cross was erected looking out over the Great Ice Barrier, now the tomb in which their bodies would drift slowly towards the sea. With their names, at Cherry-Garrard's suggestion, the closing line from Tennyson's Ulysses was carved: "To strive, to seek, to find and not to yield".

Back in England, or in New Zealand where Ory was staying with friends, the family was blissfully unaware of the tragedy that had unfolded in the Antarctic. They were busy admiring Ted's sketches that had been sent back with the relief ship or debating whether to go and listen to a triumphant Amundsen, who was already engaged in a major lecture tour following his claiming of the Pole. He lectured in Cheltenham in December 1912. The first that the family at *Westal* knew that something was not right was the receipt of a telegram on 10 February 1913, from Hodgson (of *Discovery* days), saying that the expedition had returned early due to disaster but to hope for the best. Ted's father recalled:

> The staggering blow came on the evening of Feb. 10th; I had been at a meeting of the Delancey [Hospital] Trustees and during the whole time had been perturbed by the news that the Terra Nova had arrived in New Zealand. As she was before her time, I anticipated bad news and in the evening a telegram came from May Wilson giving no particulars but sympathising with us and hoping the news was not true. Then ensued a period of suspense almost unbearable - until the truth burst upon us in all its terrible reality - the hopes of years in a moment dashed to the ground. No words can explain what our dear Ted meant to us all and to our dear, good Ory, vainly awaiting his return in New Zealand. It was a sad, sad, time.

In New Zealand, Ory was on her way back to Christchurch on the train and heard the news of Ted's death from the newspaper hawkers. She was met half way by friends concerned to comfort her and protect her from the media. In England, Hodgson had wanted to do the same for the family at *Westal* and travel to Cheltenham as soon as he had confirmation of the news. However, he could not reach Cheltenham before the evening papers were out. The entire family was plunged into grief.

Woody
Nightshade

The impact of the news of the death of Scott and his party has largely been forgotten today. The closest contemporary event for comparison would be the death of Diana, Princess of Wales. There was an a national outpouring of grief and an international media frenzy which helped to build a myth. This image of Scott and his companions as heroes has been extensively criticised but the commentators rather miss the point. The perception of a hero as someone who is perfect is as false as the modern notion of a saint. The concepts of heroism which resonated as the news broke were much older ones. Classical epic heroes often die at the peak of their worldly achievement, they die well, and they die due to their human flaws. To a classically educated generation, such heroes were Scott and his companions - a much richer and deeper concept of heroism which allows them their humanity. In this sense it was not false for the Cheltenham papers to hail Ted as "Cheltenham's Antarctic Hero", dying an heroic and noble death in the service of his country, like Scott, Bowers, Evans and Oates.

Letters and telegrams of sympathy flooded into *Westal*. Across the nation and the Empire, memorial services were held. More than ten thousand people stood outside St. Paul's Cathedral unable to get in for the national memorial service, which was attended by the King. In Cheltenham there were well attended memorial services in the Cheltenham College Chapel and in St. Matthew's Church. One of the many services held in Gloucestershire made national headlines when it was reported that the vicar of Cam, the Rev. Griffiths, died in the pulpit at Cam Parish Church:

> ...he had selected as his text Matthew X.39 'He that saveth his life for My sake shall save it' and had referred to the death of Captain Scott and his party at the post of duty, when his voice failed and he fell down the pulpit steps dead...

The Polar party, including Ted, had posthumous awards and medals bestowed upon them. Scott's final written appeal to the country to "look after our people" resulted in a huge public response which raised £75,000 (equivalent to around £4,500,000 today). From this, all of the dependants of the men who died received pensions and there was enough money left over to help found the Scott Polar Research Institute in Cambridge as a national memorial to Scott and the Polar party.

Ory arrived back in England in April 1913, having sailed home accompanied by Dr Atkinson and her sister, Constance. She went to live at *Westal* for some time. Once back in England many expedition members came to call at *Westal* and several, including Frank Debenham and Apsley Cherry-Garrard, were regular visitors. Dr Atkinson reported privately on the finding of the bodies and stated categorically that there was no trace of scurvy (often incorrectly suggested as the cause of their deaths) to be seen on the bodies - scurvy was probably incipient and a small contributory factor amongst many others. Lieutenant (now Commander) Evans lectured across the country on the expedition to packed houses, speaking in Cheltenham on 14 November 1913, when he also stayed at *Westal*. In the town, shocked by the heroic loss of one of its own, a separate memorial fund had been started to raise money for a memorial to Ted. A statue of him was created by Lady Scott (Scott's widow) and unveiled with full civic pageantry by Sir Clements Markham, in front of a large crowd on the Promenade on 9 July 1914. There was a large private reception at *Westal*. The statue was, in fact, never fully paid for and was partly an act of love by Lady Scott.

Many of Ted's grieving friends and colleagues founded memorials to him and to the Polar party: memorial windows to Ted were installed at Cheltenham College and Copthorne School, Sussex; Ted's sledging flag was hung in the Lady Chapel of Gloucester Cathedral (it has since been moved to the Scott Polar Research Institute); a Caius College flag which Ted took to the Pole was hung in Gonville and Caius College; memorial essay competitions were started in many schools, including Shurdington Village School; a memorial was unveiled at Cortachy in Scotland, placed by the Reginald Smiths; another memorial was unveiled in Norway; in New Zealand, amongst many other memorials, peaks in the Southern Alps were named for several of the Polar party, including Ted. In many parts of the world, memorials were created.

None of this, however, could bring Ted back. Ted's father thought that the insensitive reporting of such an intimate moment of their lives was deeply hurtful. Ted's loss was an immense one for the whole of the Wilson family, especially to Ory who treasured his last letter, stained with the icy film of his dying breath, until the day she herself died. Other family members also had last letters, although some received empty envelopes - Ted had not had time to fill them before he died. Ted himself would have been staggered at the fuss that was made over him at his passing and quite astonished at the deep love which his friends and colleagues held for him. Medals and statues would have flattered him - overwhelmed him even - but not impressed him. In many ways, important though they are, they only partly reflect the man. His truest legacies are, like his life, far more subtle and complex - often unnoticed in the background - and deeply interwoven, each with the other.

Firstly, there is his rich artistic legacy. A retrospective exhibition of Ted's pictures was held at the Alpine Club in London in December 1913 and was visited by Queen Alexandra and other members of the Royal Family. When the exhibition arrived in Cheltenham it drew huge crowds. Since then small exhibitions of his paintings have irregularly taken place and are always well attended. In Ted's pictures may be found not only an important historical record but a true reflection of the richness of the man. The combination of the love of creation, art, science and faith is reproduced in the accuracy, detail, and subtlety of the colouring or the pencil work and is very much a reflection of his attention to small things and of his self-discipline. He was the first to admit to artistic faults, however; his pictures were often produced under pressure or in extreme conditions and occasionally it shows, baring his humanity. Nevertheless, and perhaps because of this, his pictures still excite comment: Ted is often ranked amongst the great bird artists of his day.

Leopard Seal chasing an Emperor Penguin

Secondly, there is his scientific inheritance. The ornithological community particularly mourned Ted's early loss. In some small way we still have penguins to enjoy because of his move towards conservation campaigning. In the United Kingdom we still have grouse, in part due to his work: well maintained moors are still rotationally burned to deal with the parasite, just as the Grouse Report team recommended. It was the first report ever made into the fluctuations of a wild bird population and remains one of the most detailed studies of a disease in wild birds. For his Grouse Inquiry work alone, Ted was subsequently to be ranked amongst the leading ornithologists of the first half of the 20th century. Again, it was his attention to detail, his self-discipline, his patient observation and his determination to search for Truth in all its forms, regardless of the personal cost, which played a major role in his achievements. The records of the Cheltenham flora and fauna which he kept are a good example of this and an invaluable local treasure Perhaps this was best shown, however, through the scientific journey to Cape Crozier in the middle of the Antarctic winter to obtain the eggs of the Emperor Penguin.

The story of the aftermath of the Winter Journey has continued to develop through most of the 20th century. When the eggs were delivered to the Natural History Museum, with no Ted to lead the scientific work, interest was minimal. The First World War intervened and the penguin embryos were eventually dissected in part by three men, the final results being published in 1934. It was found that the embryos were already too developed, and too close together in development, to investigate the questions Ted had hoped regarding any evolutionary connection between birds and dinosaurs. Scientific theory moved on. Ontogony (the development of the individual) was 'proven' not to recapitulate phylogeny (the evolution of the species); the Emperor Penguin was shown not to be a primitive bird - and so the foundations of the scientific hypotheses underlying the Winter Journey were falsified. Many years later, however, in the 1990s, the link between dinosaurs and birds was made. The Winter Journey was a part of the extraordinary history of the quest for this knowledge. One small strand of the arguments used to make the link derived from work in the embryology of 'primitive' birds, such as the Ostrich. In the light of these modern discoveries, the science underlying the Winter Journey, whilst incorrect, turned out not to be so far off after all. Ted would have been delighted. He believed that every scrap of scientific knowledge, however small, was worth having. For him, the paltry result of the Winter Journey would have been worth it; taking part in the search for Truth was enough. The journey was about collecting the eggs of the Emperor Penguin for investigation, not scientific glory. Nevertheless, the Winter Journey was an extraordinary achievement, based on reasonable scientific assumptions, and its execution one of the heights of British accomplishment during the heroic age of Antarctic exploration. It has, in itself, become something of a metaphor for the quest for Truth. Apsley Cherry-Garrard, ultimately the only one of the three extraordinary men who went on the Winter Journey to return from the expedition, immortalised it in a book: he christened it *The Worst Journey in the World*. He thought that no-one other than Ted would have had the dignified patience, or the sheer moral and physical stamina to lead such a sledging journey. Scott and many of Ted's other colleagues agreed with Cherry-Garrard; only Ted could have inspired and led it; though it must be said, as Ted himself did, that it could only have been done with his remarkable companions.

Emperor Penguin

Finally, as regards Ted's scientific legacy, is the increase of our knowledge of Antarctica. Many fields of Antarctic science have been invisibly touched by him, if only through his work in encouraging others, particularly his scientific staff on the *Terra Nova* Expedition. In particular, there are reams of physiographical and geological notes and drawings in addition to his own biological work. Amongst these are the geological specimens taken from the area of Mount Buckley and carried on the sledge of the Polar party to the end. Ted knew that the party had found important plant fossils but could not know how important they would prove to be. These were the first Antarctic fossil specimens recorded by palaeobotanists of the genus *Glossopteris*, proving that the continent had once had a warm climate and providing a link to other continents in the Southern Hemisphere. This was crucial evidence of continental drift for the Gondwana theory of continental origins, a scientific hypothesis that was emerging around this time. Less was made of the specimens as evidence for this theory than could have been, in part because the geological results of the *Terra Nova* Expedition were not completely published until 1964. Nevertheless, the importance of the discovery to science would have greatly excited Ted.

Thirdly, there is Ted's medical legacy. This, on the surface, is not large. He did not occupy official medical roles for much of his life - although he never ceased to 'potter', as he would have put it, and kept up with the medical developments of his time. He did not found hospitals, like his father, leaving only a simple collection of pathological drawings, long since forgotten. Some commentators have implied that Ted was personally responsible for some of the medical factors that played their role in the Polar tragedy - as if the scientific ignorance or medical practices of Edwardian England were his personal failure. To such, he would probably have smiled sweetly and said nothing - but what could he say? He would have been the first to admit fault, if it was his to admit to. Further, for him, death was not delivered by the hands of man and was far from being disastrous. Beyond the level of such debates, however, are the many important aspects of medical work that are discreet, almost to the point of being invisible. It is the tender care which Ted took of his patients and his willingness to sacrifice himself to their needs that has proved to be an enduring example, which is still used during training in St. George's Hospital. He has proved a particular inspiration to those who seek to combine modern science with Christian care in the healing professions. Surprising though he would have found it, this aspect of the story of Ted's life has inspired others into medical practice ever since the news of his death and continues to inspire others into medical service to this day.

Finally, perhaps, there is Ted's spiritual legacy. The extent and depth of Ted's spiritual ideas were known only to a very few before the publication of the Seaver biographies in the 1930s. His ideas were not, in many ways, original but Ted was a seeker of Truth not originality: he sought to turn the teaching of the Christian Gospel and traditions (especially monastic traditions) into the reality of his ordinary every day life. As such he regularly made detailed notes on religious texts to cut through the formality and historical layering of Christian thought to make it fresh and vibrant for himself. It was the basis of his life, of his deep personal strength and moral power. It underlay his deep love of life that led him to do every small thing, every day, as unobtrusively and as perfectly as he could. To many, this simple and very private faith has made Ted an object of adulation and occasionally of derision. Many have seen him as akin to an Anglican saint. If this is meant in the modern sense of the word, to suggest that he was perfect and performed miracles, then it is false - he was simply human and made mistakes like everyone else. If, however, it is referring to saintliness in the ancient sense of the word - as one who strives to make the love of the Gospel their every day reality, serving others through this process - then perhaps; although he would have laughed at the suggestion until he wept. A small minority of commentators have dismissed the spiritual and ascetic aspect of Ted's character as showing that he had self-destructive tendencies - betraying their deep incomprehension of asceticism or even basic self-discipline. For Ted, as for all ascetics, this was always a very positive process, an embracing of a deeper Truth than the mere selfishness of the material. This type of commentator has also generally thought that Ted was sanctimonious but he was nothing of the sort. It is a sad reflection that for many modern commentators, only the spiritual aspect of Ted's life appears to have made an impression rather than his complex range of extraordinary talents. It is impossible not to comment upon it because it made Ted who he was. However, it is also crucial to realise that if you had ever met him you would never have known. Few of his contemporaries realised the depth of his spiritual life. Frank Debenham and Ted's younger brother, Jim, both expressed the worry to George Seaver and to Ory, that Seaver's books might give people a totally false impression of Ted - making him appear 'religious' - which to his contemporaries he did not - and missing his sense of fun, gaiety and laughter - which all of his friends remembered well. Debenham decided that he was probably wrong but the history of commentary about Ted suggests that he was, in fact, correct. Ted's life was taught in many schools as a part of Religious Education classes and in South Africa, for a time, was a compulsory part of the curriculum. His spiritual life has inspired very many people - rightly so - and many have tried to follow his spiritual example, as they have his scientific, artistic or medical inspiration. Yet in some ways to treat Ted in an isolated 'religious' way - particularly as a form of supposed criticism - crucially misses the very essence of him. It would be closer to the mark to sit and laugh at the sanctimony of his treatment.

Meadow Pipits

All of these legacies are interwoven - it is impossible to understand Ted's approach to his art, his science, or his faith without the understanding of their complex interactions, each through the other. His very private inner struggling with the Truth formed the foundation of his extraordinary life. It was this balancing of tensions within and without himself that created Ted as he lived his life and led to his astonishing creativity and productivity. In the deepest recesses of his being he retained the deeply sensitive and highly strung inheritance of his childhood nature but mastered himself into manhood with extraordinary dignity, quiet self-discipline and laughter. This was the basis of the deep understanding that Ted and Scott had of each other. Cherry-Garrard wrote later that Scott was the most highly strung individual on the *Terra Nova* expedition but Ory disagreed with him. She wrote to Cherry saying that she knew very well that it had been Ted. This balancing of opposites was a crucial part of Ted's creative process, the sublimation of tension into astonishing works of art, scientific insight and a spiritual and moral strength that led Ted's friends and colleagues to trust him implicitly. Few men have been so widely esteemed by those who knew them and perhaps this is the biggest legacy of all of Ted's achievements - the story of love, loyalty and friendship: human care in its highest form.

Reindeer

It takes a unique toughness to man-haul sledges and a great factor in its successful outcome is purely psychological. It is one of the greatest tests of character. Ted, Scott and Bowers were ranked by their peers as amongst the toughest of the sledgers. At the end, however, it was Ted and Bowers, the men of faith (and perhaps physically strengthened by the training of the Cape Crozier journey), who were ready to go on, to collect food and fuel to save Scott's life. As they lay dying, trapped in their tent by the howling blizzard around them, Scott wrote a letter to his "widow". In it, inspired by the friend who lay dying by his side, Scott wrote to Kathleen his hope for the future of their son, Peter: "Make the boy interested in natural history if you can; it is better than games; they encourage it at some schools." Lines that perfectly echo the strongly held views upon the subject which Ted had held since his days at Cheltenham College. From the deep friendship of two men, dying together on the Great Ice Barrier, sprang the inspiration that would forge important aspects of our modern lives through the conservation movement. Sir Peter Scott grew up to be another of the 20th century's great water-colour painters, naturalists, ornithologists and a leading conservationist; founder of the Wildfowl and Wetlands Trust, which has its headquarters at Slimbridge in Gloucestershire, and of the World Wildlife Fund (World Wide Fund for Nature). There is no evidence that he deliberately modelled his life on Ted's - and in many ways they were very different. Yet Ted, the quiet inspiration behind the lives of so many, in all walks of life, could not have had a truer legacy.

Edward Thomas Wilson died in 1918. The Wilson family remained in *Westal* until the death of Mary Agnes in 1930. *Westal* was sold shortly afterwards. In many ways Ted's parents had never recovered from his loss. Oriana died near to her home in Bushey in 1945, still a widow. She had been a frequent visitor to New Zealand and was awarded the CBE for her work with the New Zealand Red Cross during the First World War. The last member of the Wilson family to live in Cheltenham was Ted's sister, Ida, who died in 1963. The Wilson family nevertheless maintains its links with the Town, principally through the family archive deposited with the Art Gallery and Museum.

The Cairn

Top: The unveiling of Lady Scott's statue of Ted, The Promenade, Cheltenham 1914
Bottom: 'The unveiling party' in the Garden at Westal. July 1914
Back Row: (Standing) L-R Mrs G. Rendall (Polly); Skelton; Bernacchi; Mrs Campbell;
Edward Thomas Wilson; Ida Wilson; Elsie Wilson; Mrs Moore;
Mrs Reginald Smith; Reginald Smith K.C.
Front Row: (seated) L-R Miss Scott (Scott's sister); Rev. Souper; Lady Markham;
Godfrey Rendall; Bernard Wilson; Sir Clements Markham; Mary Agnes Wilson;
Apsley Cherry-Garrard; Sir Joseph Kinsey; Oriana Wilson; Lady Scott

12. Wilson Walks

*****

Love everything into which God has put life:
and God made nothing dead.
There is only less life in a stone than in a bud,
and both have a life of their own,
and both took life from God.

EAW

*****

We hope that you will enjoy walking in Ted's footsteps, discovering (or re-discovering) his home town and exploring the "little piece of Heaven" that still exists in the quiet corners of the Cotswolds.

Please note, however, that the following walks are to be undertaken entirely at your own risk. The accompanying maps are not drawn to scale and whilst we have made every effort, we do not accept responsibility for any errors, inaccuracies or omissions. These notes to the Wilson sites are provided as a rough guide only.

As a minimum, therefore, we strongly advise you to wear stout walking shoes and suitable outdoor clothing; to take a detailed map with you, especially if you are planning to take one of the longer walks; and always to watch for traffic on the roads.

Remember too, that Ted's fieldcraft was based on patience and observation. Walk quietly, with your eyes sharply peeled and you never know what you might find.

Enjoy!

Westal

- 117 -

Walk One: *Westal*

Distance and expected time: from the Museum to *Westal* (and back) - approx. 1 1/2 miles (2 1/2 kms) - 45 minutes; from the Museum to include all sites listed (and back) - approx. 3 1/2 miles (5 1/2 kms) - 1 3/4 hours.

We start this walk at Cheltenham Art Gallery and Museum (1) on Clarence Street, home to the Wilson Family collection. On the second floor a small gallery provides a display of artefacts, documents and photographs associated with the *Discovery* and *Terra Nova* expeditions. Amongst these, there is an Emperor Penguin and other scientific specimens from the *Discovery* Collections brought back in 1904; and the prayer book used by Surgeon Atkinson to read the Burial Service over the bodies of Scott, Ted and Bowers on The Ross Ice Shelf in 1913. The display also includes another book that Ted took with him to the Pole, a copy (annotated with his margin notes) of *Letters* by Samuel Rutherford, the seventeenth century Scottish theologian and preacher.

Ted's statue (Postcard c1914), The Promenade, Cheltenham. (location 4 on map)

It was Ted's father who was instrumental in establishing the Museum. In 1891 he put forward proposals for "A Museum for Cheltenham" and sixteen years later his hopes were realised when he officiated at its formal opening. When some of Ted's paintings were exhibited here in 1914, the opening hours had to be extended until 10 o'clock at night to cope with the huge number of visitors.

Just around the corner from here at 10, St. James's Square (adjoining St. Gregory's Roman Catholic Church) was the house (2) where Alfred Lord Tennyson lived. It was here where much of the elegiac poem *In Memoriam* was reputedly written, which Ted read on the Polar journey.

Also, here you will see St.Matthews (3), one of the many churches which held a memorial service when the news of the Polar tragedy reached Cheltenham. The servants from *Westal* attended to hear the Rector pay tribute to Ted's "indomitable courage and utter unselfishness".

From the Museum, heading towards the Promenade (described as "the most beautiful, because the most verdant, of English streets" in Edward Thomas Wilson's 1901 guide to Cheltenham) you'll find Ted's bronze statue (4) on the right

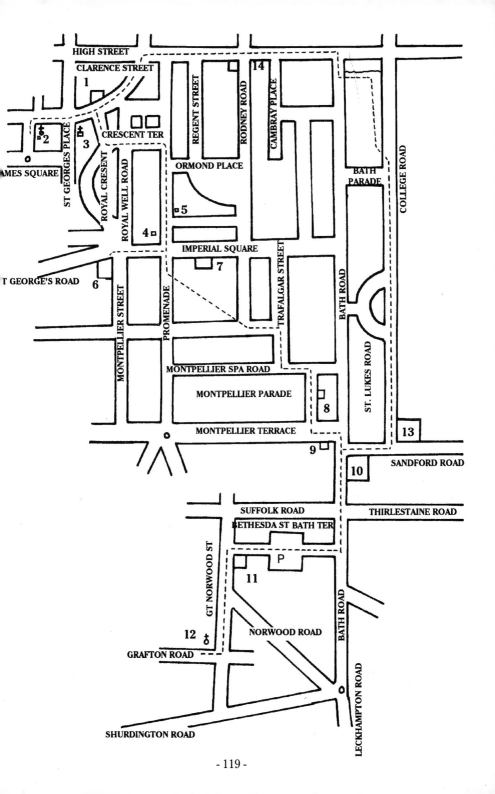

hand side. This was sculptured by Lady Scott and unveiled by Sir Clements Markham ('Father' of the *Discovery* Expedition) on 9 July, 1914. It bears the following inscription:

> Edward Adrian Wilson B.A. M.B. CANTAB. F.Z.S. Born in Cheltenham 1872. Chief of the Scientific Staff. Artist and Zoologist of the British Antarctic Expedition 1910-1913. He reached the South Pole January 17, 1912. And died with Capt. Scott on the Great Ice Barrier March 1912. 'He died as he lived. A brave true man. The best of comrades and staunchest of friends.' (Letter from Capt. Scott).

Also on the Promenade, at No. 92 (5), there used to be a W.H. Smith and Son's that contained an art gallery which once displayed Herbert Ponting's photographs of the *Terra Nova* expedition. Continuing to where the Promenade meets St. George's Road you can, if desired, detour slightly to visit the Ladies' College (6), the school which several of Ted's sisters attended and of which Edward Thomas Wilson was a Governor. It has several associations with Polar exploration, including the fact that it houses a field telephone used by the *Terra Nova* expedition, having been donated by the father of one of the pupils here.

Returning to the Promenade you will see the Town Hall (7) on your left, a favourite place for lectures and one which in the past has echoed to stories of Antarctic exploration, including from Ted himself (1906); Captain Scott (1904); Shackleton (1909); Amundsen (1912) gave a lecture about his successful Polar conquest, two months before the tragic news of the British expedition reached Cheltenham; and Commander Evans lectured here (1913) on the tragedy shortly after the expedition's return.

Walk diagonally through Imperial Gardens to reach the far corner of Imperial Square. Turn right into Trafalgar Street, left into Montpellier Spa Road and then right into Montpellier Parade. About half-way along on your left you will find the entrance to the Eagle Star car park (8). This is the site of *Westal*, home to the Wilson family from 1874, when Ted was two, until the early 1930s. The house was one of three villas pulled down to make way for the two hundred foot, thirty storey, Eagle Star building. Described at the time as a "superior villa" and "desirable first-class detached family house" you can still appreciate how *Westal* would have looked from the surrounding villas that still survive. The house took its name (which means 'west nook of land') from a small region located on the western side of Cheltenham.

No 91 Montpellier Terrace
(location 9 on map)

At the end of Montpellier Parade turn left into Montpellier Terrace. At No. 91 (which in Ted's time was No. 6) is the house (9) where Ted was born. The house dates from before 1825. The inscription on the façade reads: "EDWARD ADRIAN WILSON ANTARCTIC EXPLORER Born here 1872 Died with Scott 1912." The house is now run as a guest house and you can stay in the very room on the first floor in which Ted was born.

Proceeding to the end of Montpellier Terrace turn right into Bath Road. You will soon see Cheltenham College (10) on your left. This was the school which Ted attended from 1886 for 4 years. In the College Chapel (not open to the public) there is the commemorative stained glass 'Fortitude Window', one panel of which depicts Ted as an Antarctic explorer. A memorial tablet, also in the chapel, has the following inscription:-

> In memory of Edward Adrian Wilson, Physician, Zoologist, Artist, and Explorer, born 23rd July 1872, a member of this College from 1886 to 1891. A keen observer of Nature. A wise and trusted friend. Gentle and God-fearing. Strong, simple, and sincere. He accompanied Captain Scott on both his Antarctic Expeditions; with him he reached the South Pole on 18th January, 1912; and with him he died on Ross Ice Barrier about March 27th, 1912.

There is also a memorial tablet to Ted's 'Uncle Charlie', Major-General Sir Charles Wilson, another old Cheltonian.

Ted had fond memories of his old school and was later to return here to lecture on the *Discovery* expedition and also to give the occasional sermon. He shared the same appreciation of the "delicate tracery of the College chapel" with his father who, sleeping in Ted's room at *Westal* on 17 December 1896, was suddenly awakened by a violent earthquake and wondered how the College Chapel had withstood the strain whilst the pinnacles of Hereford Cathedral had been badly damaged.

Continue up Bath Road and turn right into Bath Terrace, through the car park until you reach the old building which has now been converted into flats and which was once St. James' School (11), where Ory was a 'matron'. From Bethesda Street turn left into Great Norwood Street and carry on to Gratton Road. On your right you will see St. Philip's and St. James' (12), where the Wilson family often attended church. This is the furthest point of the walk. From here you can either retrace your steps, carry on towards St. Peter's Church, site of the Wilson family graves and starting point for Walk Two *(The Crippetts),* or return to Cheltenham town centre via a different route following the pleasant footpath through Sandford Park and along the River Chelt. If this route is chosen you will pass Cheltenham's General Hospital (13), where Ted practised as a House Surgeon for a short period in 1900. When you arrive in the High Street you will also see the site of the Assembly Rooms, now a Lloyds Bank, (14) where, as one of the main centres of fashionable society in Cheltenham in 1898, it hosted a lecture by Nansen about his

Arctic travels. This attracted over 3,000 people, including Ted's father who later reflected: "little did we think that one day our dear Ted would be telling of his own adventures in the far South".

Walk Two: *The Crippetts*

Distance and expected time: from St. Peter's to *The Crippetts* (and back) approx. 2.5 miles (4 kms) - 1 1/4 hours; from St. Peter's to *The Crippetts*, then Crickley Hill (and back) approx. 5.5 miles (9 kms) - 2 1/2 - 3 hours.

The Crippetts from Tomb's fields (undated)

There are several starting points for this walk, depending on time and the mode of transport available; it is possible to make short circuits or half or full-day excursions.

If you are continuing on with this walk from Walk One, you should allow approximately 30-40 minutes to cover the 1 1/4 miles (2 kms) from St. Philip's and St. James' to St. Peter's Church. If travelling by car we advise parking by St. Peter's. (Alternatively, you could use one of the car parks at Leckhampton Hill or Crickley Hill Country Park as your starting point).

At St. Peter's Church enter the churchyard through the wooden arch and walk towards the church. Take the second path on the right. The church will be on your left. Carry straight on this stone path, which soon becomes a grass one, for about 100 yards (90 metres), crossing two intersecting paths along the way until you reach the third intersecting path, approximately 20 yards (18 metres) from the perimeter wall. Here, on your immediate left you will see a group of three stone crosses, the largest of which is made of granite and is about 5 feet (1.5 metres) high. The inscription reads as follows:-

IN MEMORY OF
EDWARD T. WILSON M.B. OXON. F.R.C.P.
WHO RESTED FROM HIS LABOURS
APRIL 19TH 1918
HE WENT ABOUT DOING GOOD

ALSO OF MARY HIS WIFE
D. OCTOBER 19TH 1930
SHE LOVED MUCH

ALSO OF HIS SON
EDWARD A. WILSON
M.A. M.B.
WHO DIED WITH
CAPT. SCOTT
AFTER REACHING THE SOUTH POLE
12TH MARCH 1912

The other two graves commemorate two of Ted's sisters, Helen Edith (Nellie) Wilson and Gwladys Elizabeth Wilson (see Ted's drawing of her on p.32).

Elsewhere in the graveyard are the graves of Ted's maternal grandparents and a number of maternal uncles, cousins etc. To find these, return the way you came, then follow the stone path that runs along the left hand side of the church. Carry straight on this path (which soon becomes a tarmac, then grassy one) until you reach the railings of the gate at the perimeter. Turn left and follow the boundary wall for approximately 20 yards (18 metres). You will see a large family plot protected by a railing. This is the family plot of the Whishaw family (with some members of the Yeames family). Many of the gravestones are difficult to read.

After leaving the church through the wooden arch, turn left and walk for about 300 yards (275 metres) along the main road until you see a footpath on the left beside a bungalow called *Summerfield*. The path is muddy in places and

Top end of the Bittams,
The Crippets March 31 1892

should not be attempted without proper footwear. After crossing several stiles and a small wooden bridge you soon reach Crippetts Lane. Turn left and follow the main tarmac road up the hill. (An alternative option here, as indicated on the map, is to cross the road and carry on along the footpath which carries straight on across the field and eventually re-joins Crippetts Lane further up the hill).

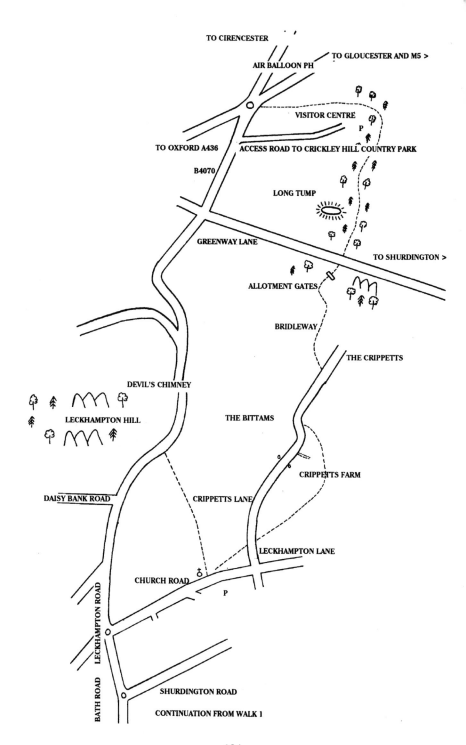

TO CIRENCESTER

TO GLOUCESTER AND M5 >

AIR BALLOON PH

VISITOR CENTRE

P

TO OXFORD A436

ACCESS ROAD TO CRICKLEY HILL COUNTRY PARK

B4070

LONG TUMP

GREENWAY LANE

TO SHURDINGTON >

ALLOTMENT GATES

BRIDLEWAY

THE CRIPPETTS

DEVIL'S CHIMNEY

LECKHAMPTON HILL

THE BITTAMS

CRIPPETTS FARM

DAISY BANK ROAD

CRIPPETTS LANE

LECKHAMPTON LANE

CHURCH ROAD

P

LECKHAMPTON ROAD

BATH ROAD

SHURDINGTON ROAD

CONTINUATION FROM WALK 1

- 124 -

On your left is The Bittams. This refers to the head of a small valley from which a brook runs down into the River Chelt. Ted often sketched from here, using Leckhampton Hill as a backdrop.

Ignore the entrance to *Crippetts Farm.*

Continue walking up the hill and pass the footpath on your left which leads up to Shurdington Hill. Immediately on the right you will see *The Crippetts*, now divided into two houses, the first of which is immediately adjacent to the road, and the second, more secluded one, which is now called *Fir Trees.* Originally, *The Crippetts* consisted of a single two-storey cottage with farm buildings. Today, although it has been divided into private dwellings, it still retains much of its original character, the cottage still maintaining the black and white timbered facade.

At the bottom of the garden you can glimpse from the road the pond where Ted nearly drowned , his legs having got caught in weed whilst trying to clear it out.

Retrace your steps for approximately 20 yards (18 metres) back to the path, now on your right, which leads to Shurdington Hill. Originally, this path (which later becomes a wider track) was the only access route to *The Crippetts*, and was used by horses and carts as well as by those on foot. Today it is a bridleway.

In 1890 Ted's brother, Bernard, had a serious accident here when his 'run away' horse nearly collided with the iron railings at the top of the hill. Although he managed to avoid crashing into the railings he was knocked unconscious for 15 hours after hitting an ash tree. The two ash and two fir trees from Ted's drawing of the scene are still there, and now much taller.

Allotment Gates, and Bernard's Tree The Crippetts
1 April 1892

Towards the top of the track pass through some old iron gates. This is the entrance to the Allotments which refers to an old, overgrown quarry, where Ted and his brothers used to play.

At this point the walk may be shortened by turning left along Greenway Lane (a place where Ted often found grass snakes). Walk along Greenway Lane and then turn left along the B4070. Passing by Leckhampton Hill on your right look out for a footpath sign-posted to Leckhampton on your left. Follow this path back to St. Peter's.

Alternatively, the path may be continued towards Crickley Hill. On your left you may catch a glimpse through the trees of The Long Tump (or Crippetts Tump), one of forty long barrows in Gloucestershire which, according to Ted's father (who presented a paper on the subject) averages 154 feet (47 metres) in length, 68 feet (21 metres) in width and 10-12 feet (3-4 metres) in height.

Long Tump and Crickley from the Allotments, The Crippetts, 3 April 1892

If the path is followed as far the Visitor Centre at Crickley Hill various sign-posted walks may be taken, including a circular route over to Leckhampton Hill. Of greatest interest perhaps is the *Scarp Trail* which leads further along the Cotswolds escarpment and incorporates the area which Ted called "the Kestrel's playground" due to the frequency with which Kestrels can be seen to hover here, aided by the upsurge of wind from the escarpment.

Leckhampton Hill from The Crippetts August 1888

To return to St. Peter's, walk back along the outward route until you reach Greenway Lane, then turn right, walk along Greenway Lane and then turn left along the B4070. Passing by Leckhampton Hill on your right look out for a footpath sign-posted to Leckhampton on your left. Follow this path back to St. Peter's.

Walk Three: Favourite places visited by Ted

Ted was always a great explorer. The map on pages 128 and 129 locates some of Ted's favourite haunts within a 30-mile (48 km) radius from Cheltenham. Whilst he invariably walked there you may prefer to drive, cycle or take a bus. The Tourist Information Office on the Promenade will have the most up to date information as to how to get to these sites. All of the locations offer pleasant local walks.

Top right:
First pointed or early English
Reliquary, north transept, Gloucester
Cathedral, September 1894

Top left:
Cowper's [i.e. Cooper's] Hill and
Severn Mouth from The Allotments,
the Crippetts, August 1890

2nd down from left:
Shakespeare Theatre,
Stratford on Avon, Sept. 1889

3rd down from left:
Ross, from the river Wye,
April 26th 1891

Bottom left:
Tintern Abbey, Wye Valley,
April 1891

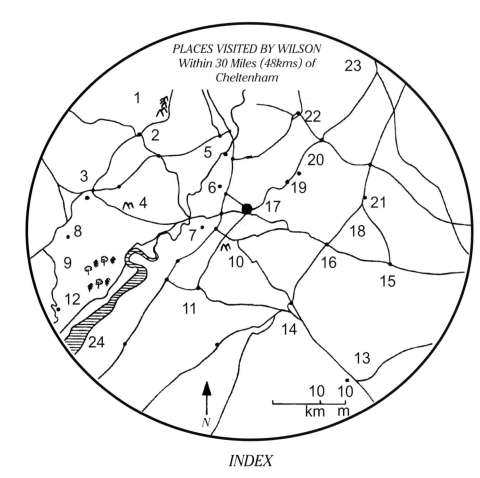

PLACES VISITED BY WILSON
Within 30 Miles (48kms) of
Cheltenham

INDEX

Gloucester Cathedral - Ted's "favourite church" - he knew every inch of it.

Coombe Hill canal - one of Ted's favourite places for bird-nesting. Now a site of Special Scientific Interest with a 2.5 mile (4 km) long footpath. The canal was abandoned in 1876 and so was overgrown when Ted used to walk here

Forest of Dean - At the Trafalgar Coal mine Ted found many fossil ferns including a huge Sigillarias 4 feet (1.2 metres) in circumference, which he was unable to carry back home. Here he also sketched Speech House which dates back to 1676.

Stratford upon Avon - The theatre from Ted's day was burned down on 6 March 1926 in a raging fire which gutted the building in just one hour. Only the adjoining museum and art gallery was saved.

Tewkesbury - Ted enjoyed sketching the unique architecture of this historic Town, which has changed very little since he came here. Sir Raymond Priestley, one of the geologists on the Terra Nova Expedition, was born here in 1886 and attended the local grammar school.

Hailes Abbey - a Cistercian Abbey dating back to 1246. It was dissolved and looted in 1539, leaving the ruins. Today, the site also houses a small museum.

Symond's Yat - the famous viewpoint at Symond's Yat rock provides extensive views of the meandering River Wye as well as, during spring, of the nesting Peregrine Falcons on Coldwell Rocks.

Tintern Abbey - founded in 1131 this Cistercian Abbey was dissolved in 1536 and its dramatic ruins have been a source of inspiration for many poets and artists, including Turner, whom Ted greatly admired. Local walks include those along sections of the Offa's Dyke path.

May Hill - this hill affords superb views of the Gloucestershire countryside, and is easily recognisable from afar with its distinctive clump of trees, which were planted on the summit to mark Queen Victoria's Golden Jubilee in 1887.

Malvern Hills - the hills rise to 1394 feet (425 metres) at the highest point on Worcester Beacon.

Walk four: Other Wilson Sites in and around Cheltenham

This walk locates other Cheltenham sites associated with Ted but which do not conveniently fit into an easy circular walk.

Scott House and Edward Wilson House, Princess Elizabeth Way, are two four-storey blocks providing 204 flats, built in the 1950s and named in memory of Captain Scott and Ted

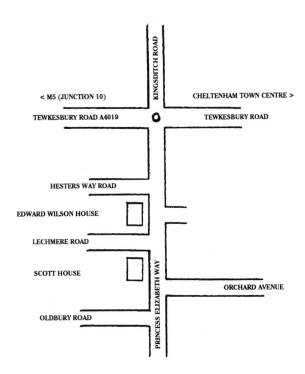

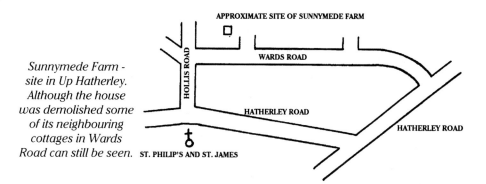

Sunnymede Farm - site in Up Hatherley. Although the house was demolished some of its neighbouring cottages in Wards Road can still be seen.

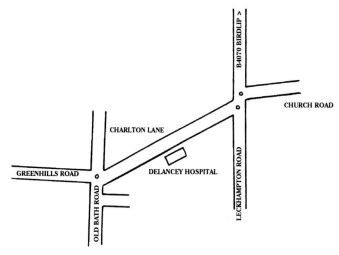

Delancey Hospital - the hospital was founded by Edward Thomas Wilson. In the original building, a block was named after him. He was attending a meeting of the Hospital trustees here, as news of the Polar tragedy was reaching Cheltenham.

Delancey Hospital

Farnley Lodge (Formerly Glyngarth School)

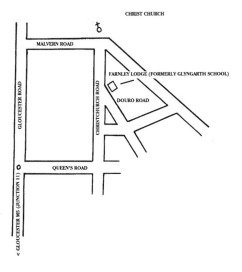

Glyngarth School. Ted attended this preparatory school for boys from 1879 for five years. In the large school room, measuring 50 feet (15 metres) by 26 feet (8 metres) Ted learned Geography, English, History, Scripture, Latin, Mathematics and French, all the subjects necessary for him to progress to a Public School. In the streets around he would fight with boys from the rival school, 'the Austinites', who were also the favourite opponents on the school's playing fields.
It is now a boarding house for Cheltenham Ladies' College and called Farnley Lodge.

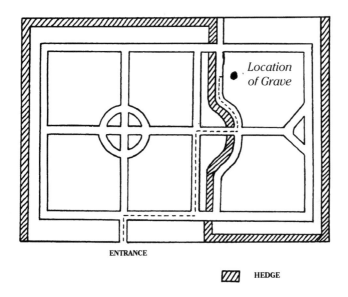

ENTRANCE

HEDGE

Charlton Kings cemetery - here you can see the gravestone of two of Ted's sisters, Elsie Violet (1878 - 1956) and Ida Elinor (1875 - 1963). They are buried together. The grave is located approx. 6 metres from the path (see location map above).

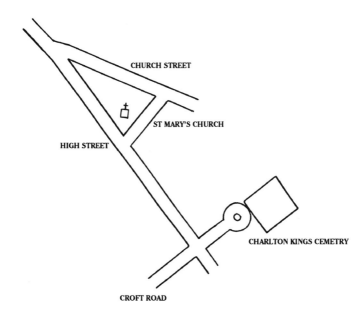

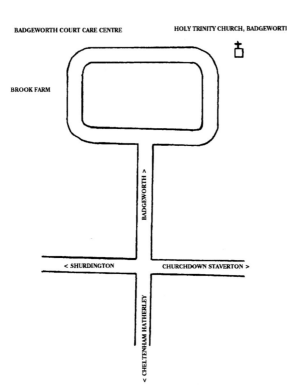

BADGEWORTH COURT CARE CENTRE   HOLY TRINITY CHURCH, BADGEWORTI

BROOK FARM

BADGEWORTH >

< SHURDINGTON   CHURCHDOWN STAVERTON >

< CHELTENHAM HATHERLEY

Holy Trinity Church, Badgeworth - in the graveyard you can see the gravestone of one of Ted's sisters, Jessica Frances. You will find it behind the church, near to the perimeter wall towards the right hand corner. It is located next to a large, ivy-clad fir tree by a compost heap. The cross simply records her short life, born on 6 September 1874, died on 2 February 1876.

Jessie's Tombstone
at
Badgeworth Churchyard
March. 1989.

List of Illustrations

Cover Design

Front: Cape Wadworth, Coulman Island © CAGM
Insert: at the Pole, 18 January 1912 © CAGM
Back: The Cairn raised over the grave 1912 © SPRI
Insert: an Iceberg off Cape Evans 1911 © CAGM

Chapter One

Chapter Two

Chapter Three

Chapter Four

Chapter Five

Colour Plates

Chapter Six

Mrs Campbell; Edward Thomas Wilson; Ida Wilson; Elsie Wilson; Mrs Moore;
Mrs Reginald Smith; Reginald Smith K.C.
Front Row: (seated) L-R Miss Scott (Scott's sister); Rev. Souper; Lady Markham;
Godfrey Rendall; Bernard Wilson; Sir Clements Markham; Mary Agnes Wilson;
Apsley Cherry-Garrard; Sir Joseph Kinsey; Oriana Wilson; Lady Scott © CAGM

Chapter Twelve

Recommended Further Reading List.

This is not an exhaustive list of possible further reading. Any accounts by the members of Scott's Antarctic expeditions are of interest. Some have current published editions. The following are the major published sources for information on the life of Edward Wilson, or are, in our opinion, reasonably reliable secondary sources.

Cherry-Garrard, A.
The Worst Journey in the World. London, Penguin Books Ltd., 1922.

Debenham, F.
In the Antarctic. London, John Murray, 1952.

Huxley, E.
Scott of the Antarctic. London, Weidenfeld & Nicolson, 1977.

Ponting, H.G.
The Great White South. London, Duckworth, 1921.

Scott, R.F.
The Voyage of the "Discovery". London, Smith, Elder and Co., 1905.
Scott's Last Expedition. London, Smith, Elder and Co., 1913.

Seaver, G.
Edward Wilson of the Antarctic. London, John Murray, 1933.
Edward Wilson Nature Lover. London, John Murray, 1937.
The Faith of Edward Wilson. London, John Murray, 1948.

Wilson, E.A.
Diary of the 'Discovery' Expedition to the Antarctic Regions 1901 - 1904
(ed. Ann Savours)London, Blandford Press, 1966.
Birds of the Antarctic,(ed. Brian Roberts). London, Blandford Press, 1967.
Diary of the 'Terra Nova' Expedition to the Antarctic 1910-1912, (ed. Harry King).
London, Blandford Press, 1972.

Yelverton, D. E.
*Antarctica Unveiled: Scott's first Expedition and the Quest
for the Unknown Continent.*
Boulder, University Press of
Colorado, 2000.

Storm Petrel